A compelling account of an extraordinary life journey. Grace's love for God and His Word will challenge and encourage you as it has done for me.

—Dr. Terry Hulbert, Distinguished Professor Emeritus at Columbia International University in Columbia, SC.

Just Grace

The Transforming Power of God's Amazing
Grace in the Life of an Ordinary Woman

Grace Jordan Hamrick

WESTBOW
PRESS®
A DIVISION OF THOMAS NELSON
& ZONDERVAN

Copyright © 2016 Grace Jordan Hamrick.

All rights reserved. No part of this book may be used or reproduced by any means, graphic, electronic, or mechanical, including photocopying, recording, taping or by any information storage retrieval system without the written permission of the author except in the case of brief quotations embodied in critical articles and reviews.

All Bible quotations bave been taken from THE HOLY BIBLE, NEW INTERNATIONAL VERSION®, NIV® Copyright © 1973, 1978, 1984, 2011 by Biblica, Inc.® Used by permission. All rights reserved worldwide.

Wedding picture by www.wearethehoffmans.com
Cover by Mary B. Bliss www.marybliss.com
"Just Grace" Scripture Reference Collage by Joshua Snipes (Grace's grandson)

WestBow Press books may be ordered through booksellers or by contacting:

WestBow Press
A Division of Thomas Nelson & Zondervan
1663 Liberty Drive
Bloomington, IN 47403
www.westbowpress.com
1 (866) 928-1240

Because of the dynamic nature of the Internet, any web addresses or links contained in this book may have changed since publication and may no longer be valid. The views expressed in this work are solely those of the author and do not necessarily reflect the views of the publisher, and the publisher hereby disclaims any responsibility for them.

Any people depicted in stock imagery provided by Thinkstock are models, and such images are being used for illustrative purposes only.
Certain stock imagery © Thinkstock.

ISBN: 978-1-4908-9995-4 (sc)
ISBN: 978-1-4908-9997-8 (hc)
ISBN: 978-1-4908-9996-1 (e)

Library of Congress Control Number: 2015916782

Print information available on the last page.

WestBow Press rev. date: 04/07/2016

Contents

Introduction vii
Amazing Grace xv

Chapter 1   Simply Grace 1
Chapter 2   Seeking Grace 12
Chapter 3   Sobering Grace 23
Chapter 4   Saving Grace 35
Chapter 5   Sanctifying Grace 49
Chapter 6   Sharing Grace 65
Chapter 7   Sufficient Grace 76
Chapter 8   Sustaining Grace 88
Chapter 9   Strengthening Grace 95

JUST GRACE

Introduction

Grace in Grace—that's what this story is all about: God's incredible, redeeming, amazing grace in me, Grace Hamrick. It is the story of a woman who, but for the grace of God, would not be around to write this book. It is also a love story, for God's grace and His love cannot be separated. God's unfailing, redeeming love is described in His Word in Romans 5:8: "But God demonstrates His own love for us in this; while we were still sinners, Christ died for us." Luke 19:10 tells us, "For the Son of Man came to seek and to save the lost." That was me—lost. And this is my story of Jesus Christ, the Son of Man, seeking and saving me.

This book is not written to point out the failures of anyone but simply to tell of God's grace. It is about God's love and the difference He made in my life, touching and transforming it by His grace and truth. Our great God is bigger than our biggest mistakes and our greatest failures. Psalm 107:2 says, "Let the redeemed of the Lord tell their story. Those He redeemed from the hand of the foe."

I wonder who will ever read this book. There is absolutely no question in my mind that God has led me to write it, but I don't know why. Is it just for me? Is recording this a healing process for me? Is it for my children and grandchildren to read about God's faithfulness to my husband, Larry, and me? I may never know, but that is God's concern, not mine.

I think about how God told Joshua to walk with His people around Jericho (Joshua 6). I'm sure they must have felt very strange doing that. How foolish (from the human view) to walk all around the city of your enemies instead of attacking. I would have felt very silly and foolish doing such a thing as that, but God had spoken, and they obeyed. I feel foolish writing this book. I am not a writer, and I certainly don't know what I am doing, but I know this is what the Lord wants me to do, so I obey and trust the Lord with the outcome. I feel like David, who said in 1 Chronicles 17:16b, "Who am I, Lord God, and what is my family, that you have brought me this far?"

From birth on, we will encounter myriad experiences that mold and make us what we are today. We have absolutely no control over a great number of these experiences. We did nothing to cause them; they just happened. We have created others ourselves. Life is a journey, and none of us know when it will end or where it will take us. Only the Lord knows because everyone's journey is different. We walk down different paths. Sometimes the path is level and smooth; sometimes it is steep, sharp, rough, and has many curves. We never go this path alone, although at times we may feel like we do. There is always One who is with us and goes before us, beside us, above us, below us, and behind us. As Job said, "But He knows the way that I take" (Job 23:10a).

The journey of writing this book began October 22, 1994—the night when it felt like the Lord reached down into the very core of my being and opened up a deep wound. I was attending a women's retreat in Myrtle Beach, South Carolina, and our speaker, Patsy Clairmont, was giving her message on hurting. While she was speaking, the tears began flowing fast and hard. I thought I was going to lose it in front of hundreds of people, but thankfully, I was able to get out of the room as soon as she finished and before I embarrassed myself.

As soon as I could leave the conference room, I walked alone on the beach in the dark for a long time, just asking, "Lord, what is going on?" As I talked with the Lord, the thought came to me to call Mr. Buck Hatch, a professor of many years at Columbia International University (formerly known as Columbia Bible College.). He was such a gentle, kind, and loving man, and in the past, I had sent numerous people to him for counseling. He was much loved by the students and everyone who knew him.

When I returned home to Columbia, I told Larry what had happened. Later, I began to question if the Lord really wanted me to talk with Mr. Hatch or if it had just been my idea. It took a very long time before I actually spoke with him, and even then, the Lord brought Mr. Hatch to me. It happened one night as Larry and I were at our friends, the Few's anniversary party. We were seated in their church, and Mr. and Mrs. Hatch sat right down in front of us. I knew the Lord was prompting me to ask him to meet with me. I don't know why I was so hesitant to do it because he was such a dear, kind man. I kept sensing the prompting of the Lord to just lean forward and ask him. I am ashamed to say that I didn't.

After the service, we went into another part of the church for the reception. Larry and I were in a corner of the room, talking with another couple, when I sensed someone approaching me. I turned, and there was Mrs. Hatch. I didn't even think she knew me, and yet the next thing I heard her say when I turned to look at her was, "Hey, Grace. How are you?"

I responded, "Fine, thank you."

Then she said something like, "What is the Lord doing in your life?"

I was stunned, and my hands flew up to my face. I felt like a child who had been caught with her hand in the cookie jar.

I said, "Oh, Mrs. Hatch, the Lord has been telling me for a very long time to talk with Mr. Hatch."

I knew this was a divine appointment. I could not believe this was happening as she took me by the hand and said, "Well, let's go see him now." Like a small child, I meekly followed her over to him.

Mrs. Hatch said, "Buck, Grace needs to make an appointment to see you."

He was very sweet to me and said to call him later in the day when he could look at his appointment book and set a time for me to come. So needless to say, I went to see him.

Before I went, I had already prayed that God would show him whatever I needed to do, and I would do it. If he thought I needed a counselor, I would go. I still had no clue what was going on and told him so. I told him what had happened at the beach, my life story, and that I didn't know why, but I knew God wanted me to talk with him. He said he wanted to really spend some time in prayer over this and asked me to come back after he had time to pray.

Several days later, I went back, and he said, "Grace, I've prayed about this, and I think you need to write a book, and the title of the book should be about God's grace. You need to tell your story about God's grace."

Because I had promised the Lord I would do whatever Mr. Hatch told me to do, I did try. I would sit at my computer and try to write my story, but it just wouldn't come. After a while, I stopped trying. This happened over and over again, and I would get extremely discouraged. But the Lord kept encouraging me. Often after I spoke at another church or taught a Bible study, someone would say to me, "Have you ever thought about writing a book?" or "I think you should write a book." This happened numerous times.

Several years later, Larry and I were talking with friends, Dave and Esther Scovill, who wrote the book *The Amazing Danis*. As we were talking, Dave looked at Larry and me and asked, "Have you thought about writing a book?" Larry told him I had been trying for a long time, but I just didn't know how. I had come to the conclusion that I just wasn't a writer, and if the book was going to be written, someone else would have to write it. Dave suggested that I record my story and let someone help me. That night, after we returned home, I told Larry we must get a tape recorder and do what Dave suggested because I felt like I was in total disobedience to the Lord.

Months later, I was having coffee with my good friends, Don and Loretta Burnett and Jean and Terry Hulbert. As we were talking, one of them said, "Grace, have you thought about writing a book?"

The other three at the table joined in and said, "We think that is a good idea. You should write a book."

I wanted to cry when they said that because I had tried but just couldn't write it. I responded by asking them to please pray for me. It reached the point where I did not want anyone else to mention writing a book to me because I felt incapable of doing it. But just a few weeks later, I was meeting a friend of mine, Gloria Wright, for lunch. I arrived at the restaurant first, and as Gloria was sitting down, she asked, "Grace, how are you doing?"

I responded, "Great!"

Then she blurted out, "I think you need to write a book!" The words had no sooner left her mouth than she quickly said, "I don't know why I said that, but I think it's a good idea."

I knew she did not have any idea that I was even considering writing a book, and I said to her, "Gloria, I know why you said that—because the Lord has shown me repeatedly to write a book, and He is encouraging me to keep trying."

As I prayed and asked the Lord to please send someone to help me, a friend, Jean Wilund, came to my mind. I wanted to call and ask if she would be willing to help me, but I wanted to make sure this was whom the Lord wanted. So when I called, I said, "Jean, I feel the Lord is leading me to ask you to do something, but I want to make sure that this is really from Him and not something I have decided. I'm not going to tell you what it is about. I just want you to pray about it and ask the Lord to show you. We will pray and then get together in a few days, and if He tells you what it is, then we will know it is from Him and not from me."

Jean asked, "What? Are you kidding?"

I told her, "No I'm very serious." After recovering from the shock, she agreed to pray and meet with me in a few days.

The day she came, we talked about a lot of things, but nothing was said about writing a book, so I decided she was not the one to help me. But I finally asked, "Jean, what has the Lord shown you?"

She told me that she had prayed for the Lord to show her exactly what it was that I wanted her to do, but she never felt the Lord tell her anything. Then she said, "I will tell you what I felt the Lord telling me when I was reading my Bible and praying this morning, and you tell me if it means anything. I was reading in Romans 1:8, 'First, I thank my God through Jesus Christ for all of you, because your faith is being reported all over the world.' It's a verse we sometimes quickly read over, but I stopped and thought, *Lord, where are the stories of people's faith today?* Why aren't we telling stories of people's faith in God and what He has done in their lives?"

I thought, *Lord, I believe You are telling me she is the one to help me.*

She then said that she had always wanted to write a book and had prayed for years about it but could never think of anything to write. However, the desire was still there. I then told her why I asked her to pray, that I had been praying for someone to help me write my book, and that I felt God was telling me she was the one.

Just as my friend Dave suggested, Jean and I sat with a tape recorder as I told her the story of my life and she asked me questions. Jean helped me in many ways, especially getting me organized and encouraging me to tell my story of God's amazing grace—even the parts I didn't want to tell for fear of hurting loved ones.

Another answer to prayer came one day while having breakfast with my friend, Dianna. She had been faithfully praying and encouraging me, and as we were talking about the book over breakfast, she said, "Grace, you need to let my sister help you edit your book—she would be great." She is an editor, so I asked her to please call her sister and see if she was willing to help. She graciously agreed. She was right, too; Erin has been invaluable. She has been such a gift from the Lord, as she has taught me how to write and encouraged me to press on.

My daughter, Fran, has spent endless hours reading and correcting each chapter and helping me stay on course. She has done a great job of helping me stick with my story.

I have seen God's faithfulness as He has provided strength and encouragement and carried me through the writing of this book. It has been a purifying, sanctifying process, as I have had to lean not on my own understanding. I also had to open up areas of my life that I didn't want to open up again. God has promised me that "I can do everything through Him who gives me strength." (Philippians 4:13)

It would be impossible to name all the people who have helped me through praying, giving advice, and offering words of encouragement. Many people have helped me birth this book. I can tell you, having a baby was much easier!

My prayer is that this book brings God glory and gives you, the reader, hope and understanding that with Him, everything is possible. There is no problem too difficult for God. There is no sin so great that He cannot forgive it. There is no life so messed up that He cannot straighten it out. There is no person so broken that He cannot mend. God is much greater and more wonderful than anything we could ever imagine. You can never go beyond the reach of God's grace and mercy.

We live in a world where there is much pain and suffering, and it is easy to feel like there is no hope, future, or way of ever changing. But there is hope, there is a future, and God can and does change people. My life is a testimony to that truth. You can come to Him just as you are because God's great salvation is all of grace.

Amazing Grace
John Newton (1725–1807)

Amazing grace, how sweet the sound,
That saved a wretch like me.
I once was lost but now am found,
Was blind, but now I see.
T'was grace that taught my heart to fear.
And grace my fears relieved.
How precious did that grace appear
The hour I first believed.
Through many dangers, toils, and snares
I have already come;
'Tis grace that brought me safe thus far,
And grace will lead me home.
The Lord has promised good to me.
His Word my hope secures.
He will my shield and portion be,
As long as life endures.
Yea, when this flesh and heart shall fail,
And mortal life shall cease,
I shall possess within the veil
A life of joy and peace.
When we've been there ten thousand years,
Bright shining as the sun,
We've no less days to sing God's praise
Than when we've first begun.
Amazing grace, how sweet the sound,
That saved a wretch like me.
I once was lost but now am found,
Was blind, but now I see. (Public Domain)

CHAPTER 1

Simply Grace

> But now, this is what the LORD says, He who
> created you Jacob, He who formed you Israel:
> "Do not fear, for I have redeemed you; I have
> summoned you by name, you are Mine!"
> —Isaiah 43:1

> Amazing grace, how sweet the sound
> that saved a wretch like me!
> —John Newton

Grace is the greatest gift you will ever receive, because it meets the deepest need you will ever have.[1]

To help you understand what God has done in my life, I need to share some of my background. Grace is the name given to me at birth. I was born in a small southern town in October 1936 to Lillian and Carroll Jordan. I was the fifth of eight children and the third girl. In addition to my parents, my family consisted of my grandmother (whom we called Nan), who lived with us, as well as five brothers and

---

[1] Dr. Franklin L. Kirksey, pastor and author of *Sound Biblical Preaching* and *Don't Miss the Revival!*

two sisters. In birth order were: Carroll, Sidney, Sarah, Anne, me, a baby who died at birth, Ennis, and Joe.

Mother, to me, was the epitome of a southern lady. She acted and spoke very properly, often correcting our grammar and telling us to sit and act ladylike. She was very kind and generous to anyone in need. While my siblings and I were growing up, she wore dresses and high-heeled shoes and kept her long hair pulled up on top of her head. People often spoke of Mother's thick, beautiful auburn-brown hair that in her later years turned a beautiful gray.

Daddy was a very successful businessman who owned and operated several businesses, including Jordan Truck Line and farms. He was also involved in many organizations, including the local Chamber of Commerce, the American Red Cross, and the Boy Scouts of America, and he was honored as Man of the Year for 1949 in our hometown. Daddy was not the kind of man to talk about what he had done. Even I didn't know what all he had accomplished until I read it in the paper after he died.

We lived in a modest house, and with ten of us in the home, there was often a lot of fussing and fighting. We were all strong-willed and boisterous. Consequently, there were many arguments over who did what to whom. We often did things we were told not to do, like skating and riding our bikes in the road, fighting, and being sassy, and consequently, we stayed in trouble with our parents. I know we gave our parents some grief because we were very disobedient at times.

As an example, my sister, Anne, and I had done something that Mother thought deserved punishment, so we were sent to our room. We had no sooner gone into our room and closed the door when we decided to climb out of the window and go play, even though we knew this was disobeying Mother. Before being sent to our room, both of us had an apple and one paring knife. This act of disobedience resulted in a trip to the emergency room. I was accidentally cut on my face as a fight between the two of us ensued over who had which apple. Then we were really in trouble.

The girls shared a bedroom, as did the boys. There was a living room and another large room in the center of the house. We also had a breakfast room that was more like a sunroom, and in it was a very long table Daddy had built in order for all of us to be able to sit and have our meals together. The table was so large that fifteen people could be seated around it, and it was so heavy that it took five or six men to carry it.

In those days, many families could afford to have help come in during the day. Mother had two women who worked every day for us and who were like mothers to me—Rosa and Dessie. Rosa was often there from the time we got up in the morning until we went to bed at night. I loved them, and they were very protective of us. Dessie did most of the cooking, and Rosa did the housekeeping. Sometimes it was like having four mothers in the house with Nan, Mother, Rosa, and Dessie telling us what to do and helping with whatever we needed. They loved us, and we loved them. If they fussed at us, it was like one of our parents talking to us, and we did not like it when any of them were upset with us.

Nan, my mother's mom, lived with us long before I was born. In many ways, she was more like a mother to me than my own. She certainly spent more time with me and was a big influence on my life. I don't ever remember doing much with my mother, but I spent a lot of time with Nan. She taught me how to drive a car, smoke, and sew. I say she taught me how to smoke because she would let me hold her cigarettes when she was through smoking them, and I would pretend I was smoking. She loved horses like I did and would often go with me to my riding lessons or horse shows. I also took dance lessons, and my dance teacher always complained when I came straight from the stables to my dance classes because I smelled like horses.

When I was twelve years old, I started driving Nan to Lancaster (an hour drive away) to visit her niece. Her car was stick shift, and she never taught me any gears except reverse, third, and fourth. She didn't want me scratching off, so she didn't tell me about first and second gear. Having Nan live with us was a highlight in my childhood. She was quite a character.

In addition to my parents, siblings, and Nan, our house also became a second home to many other children. One in particular became very important to me. I was six when an eight-year-old boy named Larry Hamrick moved to our small town. Little did I know that this boy would one day be my husband of fifty years.

Larry loved to tell the story about his first day of school. His mother decided he should wear his Sunday best, which was a knickers suit. He was placed in the same third-grade class as my sister, Anne. She didn't approve of the knickers suit and thought he looked like a sissy. To demonstrate her disapproval, she proceeded to beat him up after school.

Many years later, after we were married, Larry would always laugh and say, "I decided then, if I couldn't beat them, I would join them." As an only child, he was drawn to our large family and all the activities going on in our home, so he became a constant visitor.

Most of my childhood was marked by carefree days filled with the usual things children of that era did. One of our favorite things to do during the summer was to ride our bikes either to the country club or the park to go swimming. Both were right on the lake, just a few blocks from downtown and not far from our home. It was there that I learned to swim at a very early age, like most of the children in our small town.

We also played games like red light, giant steps, and hopscotch. We shot marbles, jumped rope, skated, rode bicycles, and played war. There was usually a game of baseball, football, or basketball going on in our yard.

Life seemed very simple then. People didn't lock their doors at night, and it was safe to walk anywhere you wanted—at least in my small town.

Daddy was the strength in our family—our stability. He was strict and ran a very tight ship, but we put him to the test. Anne and I seemed to thrive on being disobedient, and we tested him quite a bit, knowing we would be punished for our disobedience. As a result, we received frequent spankings—and I can say we deserved them.

Daddy worked extremely hard and was usually gone from early morning to early evening. Even though he provided plenty of help for Mother, he did not excuse us from our daily chores. Mother was not a disciplinarian; that was Daddy's job. When he came home, Mother would tell him which child needed a spanking. He would take that child into the bathroom, listen to what he or she had done, get a switch or belt, and really spank him or her. I know that then and now, child abuse exists, and that is sad and wrong. But we knew it was not abuse; he loved us, cared about teaching us right from wrong, and worried about our safety. After our spankings, we were sent to our rooms for a short length of time.

Of all the spankings that I witnessed in my family, only one really frightened me. We would refer to my baby brother, Joe, as the caboose, since he was the last child in the family. We spoiled him rotten, and he learned at a very young age that all he had to do to always get his way was start crying and hold his breath until he would turn blue in the face and pass out. When this happened, all of us children and Mother would be so afraid. We would run and get some water to pour on him to make him start breathing again. This happened often, and it was frightening. We noticed, however, that Joe never behaved this way around Daddy.

One night, when Joe was about eight years old, his temper got the better of him. All of us children were in Mother and Daddy's bedroom playing games. It was past Joe's bedtime, and Mother told him to go to bed. He left the room crying and then held his breath until he passed out on the floor. We ran to him, yelling, "Get the water; get the water—he's out cold!"

The next thing we knew, Daddy ran to where Joe lay on the floor, limp as a dishrag. We were standing around him, crying, when Daddy grabbed Joe by the arm, pulled him up, and started spanking him. The rest of us children screamed, "You're going to kill him, Daddy! Stop!" But Daddy didn't stop. Very soon, Joe came to and started to really cry. Daddy sent him to his room and told him that if he ever did that again, he would know what to expect. Joe's temper tantrums came to an abrupt halt that night, and so did his career of scaring the wits out of us, much to our surprise and delight.

There were a few times when I didn't get a spanking, even though I knew I deserved it. The first one happened on my first day of school. My birthday is in the latter part of October, so I was not able to enter school with the rest of my class. Daddy decided to have me privately tutored until I turned six, and then I was put into the class. I joined my class near the end of October, almost two months after that school year had started.

For some reason, Rosa was assigned the task of taking me to school. We walked the three blocks to school, crossing two streets. One was the main street leading into our town. As soon as Rosa left me in the classroom and the teacher turned her head, I got up and walked right back home, much to my mother's surprise. I wasn't there long before Rosa took me by the hand and walked me back to school. This time, I waited a few more minutes, and when the teacher turned around, I left and walked home the second time. Once home, to avoid being discovered and sent back to school, I decided it was best to stay outside.

Much to my horror, my daddy had decided to come home for a few minutes, and he saw me. I just knew I was in big trouble when he went into the house. As I followed him in, I heard him say to Mother, "Why is Grace not in school?"

Rosa quickly spoke up and said, "Why, Mr. Jordan, I've been so busy making beds, I haven't had time to take that child to school, but I will do it right now." With that, she gave me *the look*—which spoke volumes—took me by the hand, and for the third time, walked me back to school. Needless to say, I stayed that time. That was just one of many times Rosa saved me from getting a spanking.

Another time, I did something that Rosa loved to talk about over and over. I was around five years old and was walking home from my friend's house one day when I saw Mother driving off with some of my brothers and sisters. I ran as fast as I could to catch her, but she didn't see me. I was so mad that she had left me, I proceeded to march into the house and let Rosa know exactly how I felt about being left behind. They had gone to Daddy's gas station, which also sold candy, ice cream, and other goodies, and we children all liked to go there.

I told Rosa I was going to call Mother on the phone and fuss at her about leaving me, but Rosa reminded me that Daddy did not like for us to call there. I said, "I don't care; I am calling anyway." In 1941, if you wanted to make a telephone call, you spoke to an operator and told her the number.

Rosa was standing there, watching me, with her hands on her wide hips, saying, "Baby Grace, you are going to get into trouble." I told her I didn't care, and I didn't until I heard my Daddy's voice on the other end of the line. I had not anticipated my Daddy answering the phone, but much to my dismay, he did. I just knew I was in big trouble, and I scrambled to think of what to do to avoid a spanking.

At this point, when Rosa told the story, she would laugh and say, "I looked at Grace's face, and her eyes were about to pop out of her head. And then Grace just put on this sweet smile, and when Mr. Jordan asked her, 'Why are you calling here?' Grace said, 'Why Daddy, I don't remember how old I am. Can you tell me how old I am?' to which he responded, 'Honey, I don't remember how old you are. You will have to ask your mother.' And then Grace sweetly asked, 'Well, may I please speak to her?' and he gave her mother the phone. When she heard her mother's voice, she fussed at her for leaving her behind."

I loved watching Rosa tell this story. She seemed to enjoy it very much, and every time she told it, she laughed so hard, her large stomach would shake and tears rolled down her face. After I was married and had children, she loved to tell my children this story. Rosa and Dessie were very special to us and part of our family.

Other times of disobedience were more serious. One time I disobeyed that could have cost me my life was during one summer when I was working for Daddy at the watermelon platform. Train tracks ran through the heart of our town, and there was a large, covered platform in the center of it. Farmers would bring their watermelons to the platform, and Daddy would buy the melons. Then they would be packed into the train boxcars to be shipped north. I started working there when I was nine years old, as did Anne, who was eleven, and also Larry (who was now one of Anne's best friends). We worked there just during the watermelon season, and it was wonderful. We loved it and thought we were very grown up to be going to work every day.

A man named C. Rogers also worked for Daddy, and all of us loved and respected him. Sometimes he would pick Anne and me up in the morning to take us to the watermelon platform. Later, he would carry us to our home for lunch and then bring us back for the rest of the day. He helped Daddy oversee the running of the platform and the shipping of the melons, but we kids thought we were running it. Since Anne and I were often the ones getting into trouble, I'm sure it was a big help for Mother for us to be away a good bit of the day. It sure was more fun to us than being at home.

Along with Larry, there were two or three other boys his age or older who worked there as well as several men from the farm or truck line. Anne and I were the only girls on the platform. We worked from around 8:00 a.m. until 5:00 p.m., and on occasion, even much later when it was at peak season. Daddy paid me $7.00 a week, which was a lot of money for a nine-year-old at that time.

In season, Daddy was in and out of the watermelon platform throughout the day, and C. Rogers took care of everything while he was gone. There were train tracks on both sides of this huge platform, and a conveyor belt ran down the length of one side. Farmers drove to the back, and as the melons were unloaded, C. Rogers weighed them and set them onto the conveyor belt. He was so good, though, that most of the time, he could tell how much the melons weighed just by holding them.

There were boards that spanned the platform and train cars. Larry and the other boys or men would stand on these boards as the watermelons came down the conveyor belt and then load them into the boxcars according to their weight. Several men would be waiting in the boxcars to pack the melons in layers of straw. My job was to count the melons so we would know how much to pay the farmer and put the sticker on them with Daddy's logo. The logo was labeled JOGAR and had his address on it. JOGAR came from JO for Daddy's last name, Jordan, and GAR for the name of the type of melon, which was a Garrison melon. The watermelons were stacked about four or five layers, so I didn't have to put the stickers on the bottom ones—just the ones on the top layer. I would climb on top of the watermelons and put the labels on them.

Often I was alone in the boxcar while the men loaded the melons, but I felt very safe with them. They loved and respected my daddy. Many times, they would say to me, "Miss Grace, would you go up to the front of the platform for a minute? I need to talk to these melons." I knew then that they were going to say something they didn't want me to hear. They respected my daddy and would not say something in front of me that wasn't appropriate.

Well, one day, I was in a train car by myself, putting stickers on the melons. I was way in the back at the far side of the boxcar when I felt the train start to move. I knew these watermelons were being shipped up north. I ran to the door as the train moved faster. I saw my daddy, and he was screaming at me, "Grace, don't jump! Don't jump! Grace, don't jump!" Well, I jumped! I was not going with those watermelons! Later, I learned they were just moving the boxcars around, but I had been sure that I was heading up north and didn't want to go. This act of disobedience could have had a tragic ending. Daddy was very scared and thankful I wasn't hurt. Working at the watermelon platform is a happy, wonderful memory for me.

We could usually talk Mother into letting us do pretty much whatever we wanted, but Daddy taught us to obey. Obeying did not come naturally to me, but I learned there were consequences to disobedience. These experiences played a tremendous role later when I came to know the Lord, for they prepared me to obey Him. Although Daddy was a strict disciplinarian, he loved us. He was very protective, and he loved to see his children having fun. Because of that, he did some unique things for us that probably drove my mother to distraction. Mother liked lovely things and having a nice home. In spite of this, he bought a huge jigsaw table for my brothers and put it right inside the front door. That jigsaw was the first thing you saw when you walked into the house. The boys could make table legs or just about anything they wanted to with it, and sawdust often covered the floor, but Daddy didn't care.

There was another time when Daddy did something very special. We were in the backyard playing baseball, and we accidentally knocked out a neighbor's window. The neighbor was nice about it, but the next day, one of the trucks from Daddy's truck line pulled up, loaded with telephone poles and tons of wire. We all stood at the door, wondering what was going on. Well, Daddy built us a baseball field in the back yard! He put the telephone poles up and stretched the wire from the ground to the top so we could play baseball without taking out another window. He also bought a basketball goal for us and let us play Ping-Pong on the long kitchen table that he had made. He loved his kids, and it showed in many ways.

As children, we did not often have one-on-one time with Daddy, so the few times I did were extremely memorable. The first time I spent time alone with Daddy was at a banquet given in his honor at the local college. On January 20, 1950, at the annual meeting of the Chamber of Commerce, Daddy was presented with a citation for outstanding community service as Man of the Year for 1949. I don't remember why, but I was his escort that important night. I was thirteen years old, and we sat at the head table. The one thing I remember about the night was how proud I was of Daddy and how grown-up I felt. Whenever the waiter came around, Daddy would tell me to let the waiter fill up my coffee cup along with his. I didn't drink coffee, but this was his way of making sure he had all the coffee he wanted.

The only other time I remember just the two of us being together was just a few months later. Daddy wanted to see how well I drove the car. He had me drive him out to the farms so he could check on some things. I thought I was something special as I drove the car, being careful not to exceed fifty-five miles per hour on the highway. As I passed cars, being very cautious, and drove him around, he made comments about how well I was doing. After we returned to town, he suggested we stop at the local coffee shop, where the businessmen sat, visited, and drank coffee. I parked the car on Main Street, walked in with Daddy, and we sat and visited for a while.

It had been a perfect day, and I knew Daddy was very proud of my driving skills. We walked back to the car, and in my puffed-up state of pride, I proceeded to put the car in reverse without looking into my rear view mirror. Daddy immediately noticed and yelled, "Grace, watch out!" I slammed on brakes just before I backed into a car. Well, for me, that just ruined what I thought was an exemplary display of my driving skills. I drove home dejected. In my mind, I had ruined my perfect day with Daddy. I did not realize then that what would take place in just a matter of months would change my life forever.

CHAPTER 2

Seeking Grace

For the Son of Man came to seek and to save the lost.
—Luke 19:11

T'was grace that taught my heart to fear.
—John Newton

Many deaths occurred throughout my childhood that influenced my life—some to a greater degree than others. When I was around sixteen months old, Mother lost a baby boy after he was born. Because I was so young, I was not truly aware of it, but it had an impact on my life. When I was five years old, my Grandmother Jordan passed away in February 1942. I don't remember much about her. Then, several months later, another death in our family hit us much harder—that of my oldest brother, Carroll.

During World War II, we were all actively involved with the war effort. We were proud to be Americans. At some point during this time, there were some German prisoners in a POW camp near our hometown. The farmers were asked to help feed these prisoners, and in return, they would work on the farms. Mother, Nan, Rosa, and Dessie would cook hams so we could make sandwiches for the prisoners. I vividly remember working at the large table Daddy had built, along with the rest of my family, wrapping ham sandwiches up in wax paper to take to the prisoners.

My oldest brother, Carroll, along with my next-door neighbor's son, left the house one day to take the sandwiches to Daddy's farm, where the prisoners were working. Carroll was fourteen years old, and the neighbor, Ben, was twelve. Carroll was driving the car. (We could get our driver's licenses at fourteen years old.) As he drove through some sand in the curve of the road, the car flipped over. Ben was not hurt, but Carroll was thrown from the car and killed instantly. I was at my best friend's house, playing, when someone came to take me home. As a five-year-old, I didn't really understand what death meant, but I did know I missed my big brother terribly. He was my hero, and I thought he was wonderful. Everyone missed him and felt the loss. I remember lying in my bed, crying the night before I was to enter first grade that fall, thinking how proud Carroll would have been of me if he could see me going to school.

A short time later, my best friend moved away, and that was a sad time for me. I was walking home from school by myself, looking at this empty lot and thinking how much I missed Carroll and my best friend, Fran. When I got home, I asked my mother why God took people I loved away from me. I don't remember what she said or even if she answered me.

The following summer, in 1943, Daddy rented a home in Myrtle Beach, South Carolina, where we lived for most of the summer. Daddy would come down for the weekends, and I'm sure the purpose of this was to get Mother and the family away on the anniversary of Carroll's death. It was during the war, and at night, we were not allowed to turn on lights for fear of enemy submarines. The house was near the beach, and we would play war, hiding behind the sand dunes.

About the time I was eleven years old, our family suffered another death when my daddy's father passed away in 1947. I don't remember much about Granddaddy Jordan except that he was kind. He had an old refrigerator that was kept cool with big blocks of ice, and it always seemed to be stocked with great-tasting sherbet.

I was twelve or thirteen years old when our family doctor (Dr. Byerly) told Daddy that he had a heart condition and only had about a year to live. As my family explained it to me, Daddy's heart was sick; it was like a balloon that could burst at any time. We children were told not to do anything that would cause him to worry or get excited because this could cause his heart to burst. It was during this time of my life that everything seemed to start coming apart.

Everyone was very worried about Daddy, and for the first time in my life, he was home almost all the time. Daddy was supposed to rest, so Dr. Byerly (who was not only our doctor, but also a close family friend) gave him canasta cards and taught him how to play, hoping to keep him entertained while he was in bed. This is when I learned to play cards. Daddy and I played many games of canasta because I wanted to help entertain him while he had to stay in bed.

I have always thought it interesting that even though we forget many things, we sometimes remember seemingly insignificant things. One small but powerful memory I have is from this time, when Daddy was home in bed so much. I had dressed for school and walked in his bedroom to kiss him and tell him goodbye. He looked up at me and asked, "Honey, do you have on rouge?"

I said, "No, Daddy, I don't."

As I was answering him, he had reached up with his handkerchief and was rubbing my cheeks. He apologized and said, "You really don't, but your cheeks look so rosy." He did not like us to wear makeup. Why I remember that, I don't know, except for the fact that I don't have many memories of him touching me.

Like every other teenager in town, I got my driver's license the day I turned fourteen. Five weeks later, on a Friday night, Daddy let my cousin and me take his brand-new car to go to the country club, where many of the teens would often go. I had been given permission to go to the club but nowhere else. After we arrived, we saw a group of boys with bad reputations and who were not club members coming out of the building and going to their cars. I suggested we ride around for a while until we were sure they had gone. This was just an excuse because I knew they were leaving, but I was anxious to show my cousin this exciting new car that was fully automatic and had so much power.

We were on a short road when I stopped the car and suggested she slide over into the driver's seat with me and just press the accelerator to feel how you could take off without having to press down the clutch and change gears. We had only driven stick shift, and the automatic drive was new to us. As we neared the end of the road, I told my cousin to take her foot off the gas and put on the brakes because there was a curve ahead. Neither she nor I could find the brakes, and we plowed into a tree. She had a small scratch on her forehead, but otherwise, we were unhurt.

We walked to a nearby house, told them what had happened, and asked them to carry us to the hospital. I wanted to go there because Dr. Byerly lived at the hospital. (His home was adjacent to the hospital.) I was also really worried about Daddy. I was scared to tell him what had happened for fear of what it would do to him. I thought if I could get to Dr. Byerly, he would know what to do. When I got to the hospital and saw Dr. Byerly, I starting crying and asked, "How can I tell Daddy what I've done? I've wrecked his brand-new car!"

After checking us over to make sure neither of us was seriously hurt, Dr. Byerly called Daddy, told him what had happened, and assured him we were all right. Daddy sent Anne to pick us up and take my cousin home. I was so ashamed over what I had done that I couldn't look Daddy straight in the face. I cannot remember one word that he said, but I do know that neither of us slept much that night. Through the night, he kept coming into my room to check on me and then leaving, never saying a word. I knew he was worried, and I had done the very thing we children had been told not to do—worry or upset him.

I'm sure the reason Daddy kept checking on me was that just a few months earlier, a teenage boy had been in a school bus accident. The doctor had checked the children in the accident and even put some in the hospital, but this one boy kept saying he was fine—that he wasn't even hurt. Well, the next day, his mother found him dead in the bed. He had sustained internal injuries that had gone undetected. I knew this was foremost on Daddy's mind when he kept checking on me during the night. Daddy had already lost one child in a car accident. I felt horrible. If only I could undo the terrible thing I had done—if we had just stayed at the country club, as we were told.

The next morning, I got up early, fixed Daddy breakfast, and carried it to him in bed. Later, I overheard him talking to my cousin's mother, telling her not to worry about the car. He said, "We have both lost a child in a car accident—you can replace a car, but not a child." That afternoon, he bought a new car, and much to my absolute horror, made me drive my mother and sisters downtown. I realized later it was the best thing for me to do, but at the time, it was like a nightmare.

Later that day, my oldest brother, Sid, called to ask me to babysit that night. I went to his house, and after I had put my little nephew to bed, I sat reading a book. The phone rang, and it was Anne calling. "Grace, where is Sid?"

"Why are you looking for him?" I asked. I thought it was strange because I knew Mother and Daddy were home.

She said, "Never mind," and hung up.

I knew in my heart that something bad had happened—that my greatest fear had become a reality. I ran into the baby's room, woke him up, and got him dressed. Even though it was very dark outside and I was several blocks away from home, I knew I had to get there, even if I had to walk. I had started down the sidewalk with my nephew when my sister-in-law and a friend of hers pulled up. They didn't say a word, and neither did I. I knew then that what I suspected was true—that my daddy was dead.

When we pulled up to the front of my home, cars were everywhere. I ran into the house, which was now filled with people, and saw my mother sitting in a chair, wearing a green velvet dress. I fell at her feet and buried my head in her lap, crying. "I killed him! I killed him! I killed him!" My mother must have still been in shock because there was no response from her, verbally or physically. Her dress was covered in blood. Daddy had died in her arms. It was his heart, and he had hemorrhaged to death. It was December 2, 1950.

For days, I kept saying, "I killed him! I killed him!" I could not stop thinking that it was my fault he was dead. The grief and guilt were horrible. I no longer had Daddy, and it was because of me that he was gone! The only person who tried to talk with me or comfort me was one of my Daddy's sisters. Nothing she said consoled me or made me feel any differently. From that day on, my world was never the same, and neither was I. It is impossible to explain all the ways Daddy's death changed me and the impact it had on my life. I could not talk about my wreck or his death for many years, and the few times I did, I would start shaking all over telling what I had done. If I had just stayed at the country club as I was told to do, the heavy burden of Dad's death, that I carried around for years, would have been avoided.

Mother started drinking a lot after Daddy died. Nan told me that Daddy had been concerned about Mother's drinking before he died. After he died, it only got worse. It seemed that every night, my mother would drink heavily and cry for Daddy. After we moved to a different house, my bedroom was next to hers, and each night she drank, I could hear her crying and calling Daddy. It was horrible.

I know Daddy's death was terrible for her, and I kept trying to push the guilt I felt concerning Daddy's death out of my mind. But after his death, it seemed every time I did anything that met with my family's disapproval, someone would say, "You've caused enough problems in this home!"

Mother would only say, "Hush, hush; we mustn't say that, children," but since she never denied it, I assumed she felt the same way. I desperately needed to hear her say that wasn't true, but I never heard her say it. This only confirmed in my own mind that they held me responsible for his death. If I had not wrecked the car, he would still be alive.

I was fourteen when Daddy died, and from that point on, there was almost no security in my life. At that time, Mother only drank at night, and she never left the house. She wasn't mean to me during those years, but I think she was having so much trouble dealing with her loss that there was nothing left for her to give. I had no one there to help me deal with my guilt. In addition to the guilt, I was dealing with Mother's alcoholism, the loss of my daddy, and the feeling that my brothers and sisters were angry with me. My life was never the same again. It was incredibly hard.

The drinking had a terrible impact on all of us children. My oldest sister, Sarah, had gone off to college within the year after Dad's death. My middle sister, Anne, had considered running away from home. I was very glad she didn't. Anne, Ennis, Joe, and I would often meet, trying to continue keeping Daddy's rules even though he was no longer there to enforce them. We would say we were having family court, and we tried to help each other do what was right. The truth of the matter was that we were trying to raise each other. It was as though we had really lost both parents. I began to spend every moment when I wasn't at school with my friends, mostly driving around. I was very anxious to finish school and leave home.

The first time I ever confided in anyone about my mother was one summer when I was about fifteen years old. The girls in our church youth group went to the beach for a week. While there, a good friend and I went out into the ocean on our floats. We stayed close together and just started talking, since none of the other girls were around us. We both opened up and told each other about having an alcoholic parent. It was a great relief to talk about it, especially with someone who understood what my life was like and how embarrassed I felt. That day in the ocean, we were in such a deep conversation that we didn't realize how far out we had drifted until we heard a loud whistle and saw the lifeguard yelling at us, motioning us to come into shore. Needless to say, we were both very sunburned that night.

With Mother's alcoholism, Nan became my security, but only two years after Daddy's death, she died of cancer. She had always lived with us, and the void that was left with Nan and Daddy gone was huge. Before she died, Nan became very weak. She wasn't eating or drinking, so I would crawl up into her canopy bed with her and try to get her to drink some milk. When I was younger, Nan would get me to drink my milk by holding my glass with her thumb strategically placed on it. She would say, "Just drink your milk down to my thumb." As I would drink, she would slyly glide her thumb down to get me to drink more. So when Nan was getting weaker with her cancer, I would hold a glass of milk to her mouth, telling her to drink down to my thumb, as she had done for me. Nan would look at me sadly and say, "I want to so badly, but I can't. I just can't." The cancer was just too bad.

My mother had only one sibling, a brother named Ennis. (She always called him Buddy, so naturally, we called him Uncle Buddy.) He lived only two blocks from us and came by our house every day. We loved Uncle Buddy. He never raised his voice to any of us and was a soft-spoken, quiet, kind man. He had been a pilot during the war. My younger brother, Ennis, was named after Uncle Buddy, and he often took Ennis flying with him in his plane.

A few years after Nan's death, Uncle Buddy passed away, too. By the time I was nineteen, a baby brother (who died at birth), my oldest brother, my daddy, my grandmother, my other grandparents, and my uncle had all died. When I think what my mother went through losing two of her children, her husband, her mother, her father, and her brother, I can't imagine how she felt. My loss was so consuming that I had never bothered to stop and think about hers. These are things I didn't think about at the time. I'm sure all these losses contributed to her alcoholism.

I never invited anyone over, because I never knew what she would be like, and I was embarrassed. I didn't have to worry about her being out, because she never left the house. Unless someone came to my house at night, the person wouldn't know about her alcoholism. She hid it well from everyone outside the family, and I did my best to hide it, too. As time went on, her drinking got worse, and life at home became nearly intolerable.

By then, Larry had become such a part of our lives that he called mother "Mom Jordan." I didn't even tell Larry about Mother, because I was ashamed, and I knew it would break his heart. People loved my mother! Larry would come to the house, but I would often meet him at the door. He had no idea what was going on in our home. It wasn't until I was a sophomore in college and about to marry him that my sister, Anne, said, "You've got to tell Larry the truth about Mother." Unless you've had an alcoholic parent, you can't imagine what it does to you. I felt inner conflict toward Mother because when she wasn't drinking, she was fine. But when she drank, I was disgusted by being around her.

One way I was able to have friends over without them finding out about Mother's alcoholism was to have pajama parties at the shack. Years before, Daddy had built a cabin that we called "the shack" out in the middle of the woods on our farm for my two older brothers, Carroll and Sidney, and their Boy Scout friends. I'm sure when Daddy built it, he never dreamed one day his daughters would have pajama parties there.

The shack was one very large room with a fireplace at one end. There were wooden bars across the windows, and the door was a thick, solid piece of wood with a heavy iron bar that came across the door, barring anyone from coming inside. We felt very secure in the shack. However, there was no bathroom or running water. Daddy had dug an artesian well, and if you needed water or had to use the restroom, you had to go outside. One of us would stand guard at the door with an unloaded shotgun to scare anyone we thought might be lurking in the woods surrounding the cabin.

The shack was about twelve miles out of town, and my brother, Sid, did not like me taking my girlfriends out there. He would say to Mother, "Grace doesn't have enough sense not to let anyone in. Don't let her go out there with her friends."

One time, when I had taken a bunch of girls out there to spend the night, Mother sent Sid to check on us. The windows were barred, and the door was solid wood, so you couldn't look out.

Sid came out to the shack and banged on the door, yelling, "Grace, let me in!"

"Who is it?" I yelled back.

He said, "You know who it is; now let me in."

"How do I know it is you?" I asked, wanting to prove to him that what he said to Mother was untrue. Knowing he was getting frustrated, I said, "If you are really my brother, as you say you are, tell me my middle name."

He uttered a few choice words and said, "Open this door now!"

Again, I said, "Prove to me that you are really my brother, and tell me my middle name."

He kept saying, "Your name is Grace," but he couldn't think of my middle name. He went though the other children's full names but never could come up with anything but Grace for me. He finally said, "I don't know what your middle name is."

"Then you are not my brother, and I will not open this door because my brother should know my middle name." To get my point across, I told him I would *never* open the door without knowing who was on the other side. I never let him in.

When he returned home, he asked Mother what my middle name was, and she said, "We never gave Grace a middle name." As fifteen-year-olds, we got a kick out of that. My mother said the reason they didn't give me a middle name was because Grandmother Jordan wanted to give me a middle name Mother didn't like, so she just never got around to giving me one. Larry used to call me Grace NMN (no middle name) Jordan after that.

As a young child, I grew up going to the Methodist church. I sang in the youth choir. I have very few memories of my mother and daddy going to church, but they made sure all of us children were there. The only way we were ever excused from going was sickness. Even with all that time I spent there, though, I still didn't understand how Jesus could save me not only from my sins, but also from my guilt, hate, and bitterness.

In our high school, there was a teacher named Miss Rose DuPree who taught Bible classes. In the evening, she gave Bible studies for the students called Youth for Christ. I remember going one night and hearing her share the gospel. She asked all of us to bow our heads, and if we wanted to trust Jesus Christ as our Savior, to pray with her. At this point in my life, I was very concerned about death and dying, so I prayed with her.

I don't remember anything special happening, but I was determined to be a good girl. It seemed, though, that no matter how hard I tried, I failed. I always fell short of the standard I felt God required of me. I remember concluding it was impossible, so I quit trying. Although I didn't understand all Miss DuPree had taught us back then, the truths she shared with us placed a seed in my heart that would grow after many more years of looking for the answers to my questions about life and why was I born.

While these stories I have shared give you a good example of my childhood and some of my struggles, there are many stories that I have chosen not to share for various reasons. I didn't know it at the time, but God was using each thing He allowed in my life for a purpose.

The cousin who was in the wreck with me visited a number of years ago, and out of nowhere, she mentioned the car wreck. She said she had always thought we had killed my dad and that while living in Atlanta, she had been so troubled by it that she sought help from her doctor. I had never heard her say that, and we had not talked about the wreck. It was one of those subjects you knew better than to bring up. But at the moment, I wished we had. I was very glad she told me. I was sad for her that she had also suffered like that, but just having someone who understood and talked about it helped.

CHAPTER 3

Sobering Grace

Therefore, prepare your minds for action; be self-controlled. Set your hope fully on the grace to be given you when Jesus Christ is revealed.
—1 Peter 1:13

And grace my fears relieved. How precious did that grace appear the hour I first believed.
—John Newton

Though Mother's alcoholism affected all of our family, there were times she was able to control it. Even Larry, who by now had become more a part of our family, was not aware of this problem.

We all looked on Larry as a brother, and Mother had given him the nickname Bub. One day, Mother said to me, "Grace, I think Bub is in love with you."

I answered her by saying, "Mother, no . . . he is like our brother."

She said, "Well, he sure wants to know everything about you and who you are dating. I think he is in love with you."

I certainly didn't think Mother knew what she was talking about, but by spring of my junior year in high school, I began to see Larry in a different way. Although I thought I was interested in someone else, I had asked him, as my friend, to take me to my Junior-Senior prom. Even though Larry had already graduated from high school, I knew all of my friends would know him because he had been president of the student body, an honor roll student, and captain of the football team. He was a very popular and nice guy.

I will always remember when Larry came to the house that night in his white dress Citadel uniform to take me to my prom. He walked in the door, and Mother called me downstairs. As I came down the steps, I saw him standing there, and it was like I was seeing him for the very first time. My heart was jumping around so much that I thought I would faint. I quickly forgot about the other boy. My eyes were on Larry alone. I noticed that some of the girls were giving him the eye at the prom, and I let them know quickly that he was my date and to back off. After the prom, we started seeing more of each other. By the time I left for college, I knew Larry was the one I wanted to be with for the rest of my life.

I graduated from high school in 1954 and left home for college in the fall. I had no desire to go to college, but I knew it was expected of me, so I chose to attend an all-girls college in my state. Originally, my major was elementary education, but Larry and I planned to get married after he graduated from The Citadel in the spring of 1956, so I changed my major to business. This was a two-year degree rather than a four-year degree; thus, I would have something to show for my time in college.

For the most part, I enjoyed college life and especially enjoyed attending summer school between my freshman and sophomore year to take courses that would allow me to catch up with the other two-year business students. During my freshman and sophomore years, I often drove to Charleston on the weekends to be with Larry. There was always a group of us going, and often, we would stay at beautiful old homes on the Battery. What a treat! We would all wear our formal dresses with the big hoops underneath, and when we stayed at these homes, it was like a scene out of *Gone with the Wind*.

I especially felt this way when our cadets arrived in their white dress uniforms and we would parade down the huge spiral staircases.

Larry gave me a diamond ring during the summer of 1955. We planned to marry on June 9, 1956, just after he graduated from The Citadel. Even though I only had one semester left, I talked my mother into letting me come home the last semester of my sophomore year to attend a local college and help with my wedding. In December 1955, my sisters (Anne and Sarah) became engaged and planned to marry sometime during the summer of 1956 as well.

Spring of 1956 was an exciting time for all of us, especially for Larry and me as we planned our wedding. Just a few weeks before my wedding, Anne informed Mother that her fiancé, George, had some leave time from the Navy and wanted to marry her then. The new date set for their wedding was Sunday, June 3, only six days before ours.

Our house became a whirlwind of activity as we put my wedding on hold and started planning Anne's. My sister, Sarah, decided to get married in July, so Mother had three weddings in six weeks. In the end, it was good that I had talked Mother into letting me come home that semester to help with everything.

It was a custom then to display wedding gifts in a room in your home. Our gifts had already starting arriving, so Larry and I had to pack up our gifts and put them away to make room for Anne's. There was also some confusion, as gifts would get mixed up in all of the rush when they arrived at the house. Anne was to have been one of my bridesmaids, and this was no longer possible. In addition to all of the changes, there were the last-minute parties, fittings, and the flurry of activities that surround a wedding.

By the day of my wedding, I was just about a wreck. I remember telling Larry's mom just minutes before I was to walk down the aisle that I thought I was going to throw up. She looked at me and said, "If you do, I'm going to spank you." We both had a good laugh over that for many years.

In spite of all the craziness before the wedding, everything went really well. My twenty-six-year-old brother, Sid, gave me away, and had told me that he was not going to wear shoes. He was so serious that I fully expected him to show up barefooted, but much to my delight, he had on shoes and looked quite nice in his tuxedo. When I walked down that aisle and saw my wonderful husband-to-be, I thought my heart was going to burst. This was the happiest day of my life.

We honeymooned at a resort in Tennessee but spent our wedding night in Columbia, South Carolina. We soon realized that in all the confusion, we had left home with very little money. That night, we had just enough to buy two hamburgers and split a milkshake. The next day, Larry's dad wired money to us. We had many laughs through the years over how we started out with no money, just lots of love.

Upon graduating from The Citadel, Larry was commissioned as a lieutenant in the Air Force. We knew he would be going into the Air Force the following February, and we would be required to move to San Antonio, Texas for his training. During the eight months between graduation and our move to Texas, we lived in Columbia. Those first few months of marriage were not anything like I had expected. I loved Larry dearly, but both of us had some rough times.

It was summer, and summertime in Columbia, South Carolina is extremely hot. We lived in a one-bedroom apartment with no air-conditioning. It was so hot that we were miserable and couldn't sleep. We had a very tiny kitchen, and for some crazy reason, I thought I had to cook for Larry, as I had seen Dessie cook for us. Every morning, I would get up and fix Larry a big breakfast before he left for work. He came home for lunch every day, and so right after breakfast, I would start preparing our noon meal. Growing up, we mostly ate meals, not sandwiches, so I cooked meat and vegetables. Sometimes I would buy fresh corn and shell fresh butter beans or peas, just like I had seen Dessie do. Larry would come home and eat, and it seemed it would take me from lunch to dinner to clean up and then start preparing another meal. Day after day, this went on until after several months, Larry came home and found me in a pool of tears.

"I can't do this anymore. I am so tired of being in this hot, tiny kitchen, cooking," I cried.

He looked at me and said, "Oh, honey, I am so glad to hear you say that. I have been miserable, and I didn't want to hurt your feelings, but I would still be so full from all the food at lunch that I dreaded coming home to eat again."

Not wanting to hurt my feelings, he was eating everything I had prepared and had gained twenty pounds in just a few months. He was gaining weight, and I was getting thinner. I was five feet, five inches tall and weighed 109 pounds. I was miserable, and so was he.

By this time, it was near the end of September. We settled down to a more normal cooking routine, and the weather cooled off some. Finally, we were able to have fun and just enjoy our time together before entering the Air Force. In October, I found out I was pregnant, and we were both thrilled over the prospect of having a baby. During my first visit to the obstetrician, the doctor did some blood work and discovered I had a negative blood type. He told me, "You can have one baby safely, two maybe, but three could be a risk because of your RH factor." As he explained it, when a woman with an RH-negative blood type has a child with the same RH factor, there isn't a problem, but when the baby is RH positive, it becomes a major health issue for the baby. So as long as you had babies with negative blood, there was no problem.

I wondered if my mother also had negative blood. Then I thought that perhaps this had been the cause of the death of Mother's baby when I was about sixteen months old. I went to Mother and asked, "Tell me what happened to the baby that died between Ennis and me."

She said, "Honey, you had an ear infection, and you were burning up with fever. I was holding you, and you kicked me in the stomach. The doctor said that's what killed the baby."

I just looked at her. I could not believe what she was saying. My mind told me that no sixteen-month-old could be responsible for that, but this just added to the guilt I felt over my wreck and

Dad's death. I know my Mother couldn't have known how her words affected me, but I could not get them out of my mind.

After Larry completed his training in San Antonio, we moved to Houston, Texas where our daughter, Debbie, was born in May 1957. After a year in Houston, we were transferred to the Air Force base outside of Nashville, where our second daughter, Fran, was born in April 1959 in Murfreesboro, Tennessee. Larry finished his three years in the Air Force, and we moved back to Columbia, South Carolina where in August, 1963 our third daughter, Sandra, was born.

Larry and my three girls were my joy and delight. We moved into a wonderful neighborhood with a lot of young families with whom our girls could play. Larry and I would often take the children to the beach and on trips during the summer when they were not in school. Everything just seemed to be perfect except for occasional childhood sicknesses. Larry and the three girls meant more to me than anything. I was determined to be the best mother and wife and never do anything to hurt my children. I wanted them to be able to come to me for anything at any time, and I wanted them to know that no one was more important to me than they were.

In time, I began to experience a lot of stress as a young mom raising three young children—often by myself, as Larry's job required a lot of traveling. Things within me began to change, and I found myself having trouble making even simple decisions. Over the next few years, I had several crazy things start happening to me physically. I had major panic attacks and would start shaking for no reason. I reached the point where I was having difficulty just doing ordinary tasks. A little thing, like making a phone call or going somewhere, would trigger a panic attack. No one would have guessed that I had any problems because I didn't act as though anything was wrong, but physically, things started changing.

In the spring, when I was in my late twenties, I knew I needed help, so I went to my doctor. He asked what was going on with me because my blood pressure was so high. He started asking a lot of questions and was so concerned that he called Larry at home.

The doctor told him he wanted to put me in the hospital because he knew something was going on, but he didn't know what it was. They admitted me to the hospital for about a week but couldn't find anything wrong. The doctor told Larry he wanted to call in a psychiatrist while I was still in the hospital. The psychiatrist asked me all kinds of questions. It seemed like I cried the whole time I was there, though I didn't know why.

The psychiatrist decided I needed to go on medication and see him on a regular basis. Emotionally, I got worse after that. The period of time from when I was twenty-nine to thirty-six years old is like a blank period in my life. Secretly, I wanted to die. I kept hearing a voice that said, "If you really loved Larry and your girls, you would kill yourself because you're just a bad person—you harm people."

Those thoughts went through my head many times. Even as I am writing this, I realize how hard it is to believe that a person can buy into these lies and reach this point, but I did. I would sometimes do crazy things. A couple of times I took Valium along with an alcoholic drink, hoping that I wouldn't wake up. It was at night, after the children had gone to bed. Larry was there, but he did not know what I was doing. There were several times it seemed my heart would barely beat because I had so many tranquilizers along with alcohol in my system. All this didn't happen overnight but rather over a period of time. Unless you have been in the midst of a deep depression, you can't imagine how horrible it is. Your thinking is so confused that you really don't know what is going on or why you feel the way you do.

The doctor put me on anti-depressants and tranquilizers, and I began drinking more almost every day. No one would have ever known it unless that person really knew me. I only drank in the late afternoon and evening. Larry knew I drank, but he didn't realize how much. I was becoming more miserable every day, and I knew Larry was, too.

During this time, my college roommate, Jean, came to see me and realized how much I had changed. She started crying and said, "Grace, you are no longer the person I knew. Please get off this medication." I knew she was right, but I was afraid to stop taking it. The medications changed me drastically.

One day, I decided I wanted to go back to my hometown to see my old family doctor and talk to him about Daddy's death and the death of Mother's baby. I went to Dr. Byerly and asked him to tell me what caused Daddy's death.

He said, "Your daddy had a heart condition. If it had happened about ten years later, we could have operated and saved him, but we didn't know how to do surgery for it at that time."

I knew that Dad was told to stop working so hard, rest, and avoid excitement. Then I asked him about Mother's baby who had died. "What killed that baby?"

He looked at me and asked, "Grace, why are you asking me these questions?"

I told him that I was under the care of a psychiatrist and that I always felt responsible for my daddy's death and felt that my family held me responsible, too. I also told him that when I had talked with Mother about the baby who died, she said he had told her that my kicking her in the stomach had killed the baby.

"Grace, I never told your mother that. That baby died . . ." He rattled off all the things that were wrong with the baby and why he had died. It turns out the baby could never have lived. I don't know if Dr. Byerly just told me this to try and help me, but I chose to believe him.

Finally, the turning point came when Larry and I had flown out of town to visit some friends. Before we left, I decided that while I was there, I was not going to take any medication. We were there for the Mardi Gras weekend, and I knew we would be partying.

The night we returned, I went on what my doctor called a drug withdrawal trip. I was scared to death. I felt like I was being sucked into a black hole, and I was fighting to keep from being drawn into it. I sat on our bed and kept begging, "God, please don't let me go." I felt that if I stopped saying those words, I'd get sucked into this dark place. I wouldn't let Larry leave my side. Larry sat there, holding my hand, while I said those words repeatedly: "God, please don't let me go." Then I said to God, "If you will keep me from going into this black hole, I promise I will do something about all the medication I'm on." I was so bad off that night Larry had to call my psychiatrist. The psychiatrist told Larry what medicine to give me to settle me down, and I finally fell asleep.

This was a wake-up call. It had a sobering effect on me, and I never wanted to go through that again. I had made a promise to God that I would try to do something about the medication I was taking, so I went to see my psychiatrist. I was anxious but absolutely determined that I was going to get off all the medication. When I told him what I wanted, he said, "Grace, if anything, I am going to increase the dosage. You are not doing well."

I said to him, "I understand there is a place here in the city that treats patients without a lot of drugs. I want to go there." In essence, I was telling him that I was quitting him.

He said, "Well, I can't tell you not to do it."

I asked him if he would take me back if they couldn't help me, and he said he would.

That day, I called and made an appointment to see if this group of psychiatrists who did not administer a lot of drugs, could help me. They told me they thought they could but they wanted me to bring somebody who was close to me, so naturally, Larry went with me. I was around thirty-six years old at the time.

On the day of my first appointment, they ran a battery of tests and interviewed both Larry and me. One of the doctors was a woman, Dr. Jones (not her real name). I really connected with her and wanted her to be my doctor. At the end of the day, they called me into a conference room. There were many people sitting around a large oval table, some of whom I didn't know. They asked me why I wanted to come there. I said, "Because I feel like I am in hell, and I want out." They asked me all kinds of questions and told me they wanted me to come as an outpatient because they felt I wasn't a threat to myself. I asked if I could have Dr. Jones as my doctor, and they said yes.

Dr. Jones gradually got me off all the medication the other psychiatrist had me taking. She met with me alone at first and then with Larry. I continued to see her weekly as an outpatient for at least a year. She then discharged me, saying, "Grace, I think you're okay now. You've come a long way since we first saw you."

A couple of years later, I went to visit her—just as a friend. She was extremely pleased by how well I was doing and told me that the doctor who was the head of the psychiatric department when I first came had said of me, "She is going to be a hard nut to crack." She said no one wanted me as a patient because none of the other doctors thought they were going to be able to break through and help me. They said I had built walls so thick to protect myself, none of them thought they would be able to bring them down. But Dr. Jones helped me to function without medication.

I was better emotionally, but I still carried guilt over my dad's death. I was managing successfully without medication but continuing to drink—though not as heavily as before. I had a friend, Susan (not her real name), who often came over to my house. We sat around the kitchen table in the late afternoon and drank. As I look back, I can see how God was weaving everything that was happening in my life like a tapestry because the timing was perfect.

Susan and I sat there, drinking, smoking, and talking, and I'd ask, "Susan, did you ever stop and think why you were born?" You see, this was a big thing for me because if there was a God—and I believed there was—then there had to be a purpose for being here. I would say to her, "If there is a God, there has got to be a reason why we're here. Surely God did not create people just to be happy and to live a good life. There has to be more than this."

I certainly knew a lot about God because I'd gone to Sunday school and church all my life and even called myself a Christian. Because I grew up in the church, there was never a time in my life when I did not believe in God. As a child, whenever I was afraid, Mother would tell me, "Grace, don't be afraid. God is going to take care of you."

As Susan and I sat and drank, I couldn't imagine that this life I was living was all God intended it to be. I didn't think God would create people with no purpose for their lives. I thought surely we weren't created just to do the best we could, find happiness where we could, and just go our own ways. There had to be a purpose for living. Even though I had a wonderful husband and three wonderful children, I felt there had to be more to life.

Not too long after, Susan moved out of state. During the next five years, she wrote to me, and I noticed a change in her letters. She began talking about the joy and peace she had found. She started writing and quoting Scripture to me. She often told me, "I love you so much. I want you to know the joy and peace that I have found."

Over those five years, she faithfully wrote me four or more typed pages, quoting Scripture and telling me how much she loved me and God loved me. Susan now had me reading my Bible, but I was still miserable a lot of the time. It seemed there was a battle going on inside of me. God began to move in my heart, though, as I read her long letters telling me of God's love and grace.

Susan sent me a little booklet that explained how Jesus Christ died on the cross for us and that Christ's death had paid for all our sins. I also began to understand that Jesus came to cleanse me of my guilt. When I sat in my room, reading those words, I felt a ray of hope. The guilt I had carried over the years was too much to bear. I was slowly beginning to understand the truth of what Christ had done for me, and it was like a beam of sunlight shining on me. I had always known about God and that Jesus Christ had died on the cross for my sins. I had known this all my life, but it was just head knowledge.

Around this time, Larry and I attended a weekend retreat at our church where people were asked to share their testimonies. Larry believed he was saved as a teenager, but his life did not change until after this retreat in 1974. On a Sunday afternoon, Larry went into our bedroom alone and got on his knees by the bed. He told the Lord, "I know you are my Savior, but I want you to be Lord of my life." He said that in the past, he had tried to make every kind of deal he could think of with the Lord—giving God 90 percent of himself and keeping 10 percent—but nothing worked until that Sunday afternoon, when he finally said, "God, I want you to have 100 percent of me and be Lord of my life." Larry's life really changed that day.

Soon after that, he quit drinking and smoking, and that bothered me. I had lost my drinking and smoking buddy. I was angry. How could I fight God? My husband had changed because God had changed him. For about a year and a half after that, I felt like Larry was trying to change me, and I rebelled like crazy. He went to church all the time and pressured me to go, too. The more he did, the more I resented it and would sometimes say no just because I felt he was pressuring me.

All this time, Susan continued writing to me. In the meantime, God began dealing with Larry concerning me. Larry said that one day, God impressed upon him, "You're trying to play the Holy Spirit with Grace, and I'm not going to do one thing with her until you get yourself right with Me as far as loving her biblically. When you love her biblically and unconditionally, then I'll start working in Grace." So Larry started loving me unconditionally, and when he did, God began to soften my heart. Larry began showing me how the grace of God is manifested in a life.

Everything was to come together in April 1976. The best was yet to come.

CHAPTER 4

Saving Grace

> That if you confess with your mouth, 'Jesus as Lord',
> and believe in your heart that God raised Him
> from the dead, you will be saved. For it is with your
> heart that you believe and are justified, and it is
> with your mouth that you confess and are saved.
> —Romans 10:9–10

> I once was lost but now am found,
> was blind but now I see.
> —John Newton

Susan continued writing to me about God's love, grace, and mercy, but I still struggled with God—and the more I did, the worse I felt. Poor Larry was doing everything he could to help me. Around this time, she came and stayed with me for a few days. When I mentioned this to another friend, she asked if she could bring two of her friends over to talk with her. I asked Susan, and she said she would be glad to talk with them.

On the day they were coming, I explained to Susan that I would prepare lunch for all of them, but I didn't want to be in on their conversation. I knew they were going to be talking about God, and I didn't want to hear it. I had the table set and lunch prepared when they arrived. After welcoming them, I told them I was going into Larry's office to do some work for him while he was out of town. Before I left, Susan looked at me and asked, "Do you have to go?"

I got upset because I had made it clear to her that I didn't want to stay and listen to what they had to say. I looked at her, said, "Yes, I do," and marched out of there.

I went out into the office, which was a room attached to the garage. While I sat there, trying to get some work done, my conscience bothered me. I thought, *Grace, Susan loves you so much, and all she wants is for you to sit with them as they talk.* I battled with this thought. Finally, I just grabbed my pack of cigarettes and marched back into the house. I found them, of all places, downstairs in the sitting area of our bedroom. The women watched as I sat down on the carpet in the doorway of our bedroom. I wasn't going all the way into the room, because I was trying to distance myself from this religious conversation. I sat there, listening to Susan talking to the women. One of the ladies was confessing something she was doing that was not good. I sat in the doorway a little away from them, puffing away on my cigarette, thinking, *Grace Hamrick, you think you are so bad, but you haven't done that.*

What happened next is difficult to describe, but I had no sooner had that thought when it seemed as if God reached down, grabbed me, and said, "Grace, you and I are going to have a talk." It felt like He shut me up in a soundproof booth with Him because even though I was so close to them that I could almost touch them, I didn't hear a word they said.

All the Bible verses that I had been reading for months flooded my mind. God was speaking to my heart, and I knew He was saying to me, "Grace, you say you know Me, but your heart is far from Me! You are so busy comparing yourself to everyone else because you are always trying to find somebody else that you feel is worse than you. It is not about you and them. It is between you and Me. I am a Holy God, and you have sinned against Me."

Romans 12:1–2 came to my mind and I thought about what Christ had done for me on the cross. The next thing I knew, I felt like there was a searing hot iron behind my eyeballs. I know it sounds strange, but the tears streaming down my face felt incredibly hot. I felt deep conviction in my very being. It was like God was saying, "You have offended Me." A deep sadness came over me. I was so sorry for all the wrong I had done.

I knew at that moment that God was speaking to my heart. I knew God was saying, "Grace, I want you. Will you let Me come in? Will you trust Me with your life?"

I struggled with that, as I had many times before because I did not want to give up control of my life. Immediately, thoughts came into my head of what it would mean if I gave my life over to God. The first was, *If you do that, Grace, you're going to be sent to Africa.* Then I remember thinking, *Then so be it. If that is what God wants of me, then I'll do it.*

Then the next thought that came was, *If you do that, you're going to die. Larry's going to die, and your children are going to die.* As I look back on it, I can see the battle that was going on with Satan whispering these horrible thoughts into my head. I said, "Well, God, You are either who You say you are, and I'm going to trust You with the lives of my husband, my children, and myself, or there is no hope at all."

I knew God was saying, "Grace, trust Me."

I prayed, "God, I want You more than anything."

Revelation 3:20 says, "Here I am! I stand at the door and knock; if anyone hears My voice and opens the door, I will come in and eat with Him and he with Me." That moment, I said, "Lord, please come into my life and be my Lord and Savior. I need You."

No bells rang or anything like that. Instead, I felt like the huge battle that had been going on in my life was finally finished. I had been struggling with God for a long time. But it was over.

After I prayed, I said, "God, I can't quit drinking, cussing, smoking, or change my life. I really am a basket case. But I'm not mine anymore; I'm yours, and if anything is going to come of my life, You are going to have to do it. I can't; I have tried."

Then a thought popped into my mind. *Grace, can you put out that cigarette?* I thought, *Yes, I can do that*, and I put out the cigarette.

After that, it was as if the soundproof booth door opened, and I heard one of the women say, "I've got to go."

Susan said, "Well, before you do, let's pray."

I asked Susan to pray that God would take everything in my life that was displeasing to Him away from me. She started praying. She was crying and saying, "God, I have prayed for this for years!"

I thought, *I haven't told her what I have done! How does she know that I prayed to receive Christ?* Well, she just knew, and she was thanking God for answered prayer.

Larry was out of town that day, and I couldn't wait to call and tell him what I had done. I called him at his hotel and told him what had happened. Later, he told me that after we hung up, he broke down and cried.

Our marriage changed forever after that. God began to teach us through His Word what a biblical marriage looked like as we began to apply the truths we heard and read in the Bible. We had twenty years without Christ in our marriage and thirty with Christ, and there is a world of difference—like moving out of the darkness and into the light.

From that moment on, my life changed drastically. The most notable change was that He took away the hold that alcohol and cigarettes had on me. I have never touched another drop of alcohol or smoked another cigarette after that moment. It was all God—He totally took the need for those things away. Only someone who has been addicted to either or both of those substances could understand what a great gift it was to have that prayer answered instantly.

Was I ever tempted to smoke or drink again? Yes—many times. But each time, I would cry out to God to keep me from giving in to the temptation, and He always—without fail—answered my prayer.

The first thing I did was throw every pack of cigarettes I had into the garbage. Then I poured every bottle of alcohol in the house—and there were plenty—down the drain. I really meant business, and I did my part by getting rid of these temptations. I trusted God to do the rest, and He did. God began to change me in many ways.

Another big change was how the Bible seemed to transform before me. In the past, I would try to read my Bible, and it made no sense. But after that day, God put such a hunger in me for the Word that I couldn't seem to get enough. I began to understand things I had never understood before. When I read about God parting the Red Sea and other miracles in the Bible, I don't hesitate to believe them, because I know the miraculous things God has done and is doing in my life. Those were just the beginning changes. Then He began bringing people across my path to help me grow as a Christian.

The most incredible journey of my life had just begun.

Grace's grandmother, Nan, holding Grace's mother. 1904

Grace as a baby and her older siblings April 1937

Grace being held by her oldest brother,
Carroll, who was killed. 1938

Grace in the boxcar working at her
Dad's watermelon platform. 1946

Grace as a cheerleader 1953/54

Grace while at Columbia College 1955

Larry and General Mark Clark at The Citadel 1955/56

Larry and Grace Homecoming at The Citadel 1955

Grace and Larry's wedding picture June, 1956

Larry in the Air Force 1958

Larry and Grace's three daughters Christmas 1965

Our three daughters fishing 1972

Larry and Grace with grandkids 1994

Larry and Grace 1988

Larry and Grace on a "Grand" trip 1999

Our family, Christmas 2005

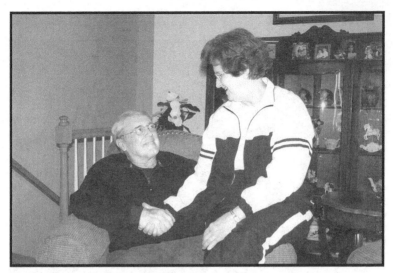

Larry and Grace six weeks before Larry's death 2006

All of the family at our grandson Bradley
and Courtney's wedding 2013

CHAPTER 5

Sanctifying Grace

> May God himself, the God of peace, sanctify you through and through. May your whole spirit, soul and body be kept blameless at the coming of our Lord Jesus Christ. The One who calls you is faithful, and He will do it.
> —1 Thessalonians 5:23–24

> The Lord has promised good to me,
> His Word my hope secures.
> —John Newton

> "Sanctification means being made one with Jesus so that the nature that controlled Him will control us."
>
> "Are we prepared to say, 'Lord, make me, a sinner saved by grace, as holy as You can?'"
>
> —My Utmost for His Highest
> Oswald Chambers (February 8)

I believe God uses all the circumstances in our lives to help us see our need for Him as our Savior. After we have trusted Him as Lord and Savior, I believe He uses everything that touches our lives to conform us into the image of His Son (Romans 8:28–29). This is the process of sanctification, and it takes a lifetime.

For me, this all began when the Lord brought a dear lady into my life to get me grounded in biblical truth and help lay a lifelong foundation for His Word. I heard about a Bible teacher, Vivian Boyd, for many years before I came to know the Lord, and although up to this point, we had never met, that would soon change.

I had a friend call me with problems, but as a brand-new believer, I knew they were beyond my ability to advise her. I shared with her what God had done in my life and how He had radically changed me. Then I gave her Vivian's name and suggested she get in touch with her, which she did.

Some time earlier, I had shared my testimony with some of my friends whom I had played cards with. I told them what God had done in my life and that all I wanted to do was learn more about Him and study the Bible. A couple of them called the next day and asked if they could study the Bible with me. I said yes, and that began my first Bible study.

I used a small study booklet on the gospel of Luke called *Neighborhood Bible Studies*, that my sister, Anne, had given to me. The ladies and I sat around my kitchen table, studying the Bible. I felt very awkward praying out loud, and I hardly knew anything—I certainly didn't know how to lead a Bible study. I would read the question in the booklet, and we would look up the answers in the Bible. I felt like the blind leading the blind.

One day, this friend (the one whom I gave Vivian's name) called and said she wanted to bring Vivian to the Bible study. When we met, I liked her immediately, and that was the beginning of a lifelong friendship. She lived around the corner from me, which was very convenient, and we started getting together. I could talk to her about anything, and I always felt totally loved and accepted by her. I had a hunger for God's Word, and she enjoyed teaching me as much as I enjoyed listening and learning.

Over the years, we would walk around our neighborhood and talk about the Lord while we were getting our exercise. The children would laugh when I would say, "I'm going to Vivian's for a few minutes." My girls' response was, "Yes, Mom; we'll see you in a few hours." Whenever we were together, time would fly by as we studied the Bible.

For over thirty years, Vivian was a part of my life. She was like a mother, sister, and best friend all rolled into one. She would sit and listen to everything I had to say, and by the time I left, she had taken the Word of God and totally turned me in the right direction. I could then focus on what the Lord would want me to do. I knew she loved me, and I never felt condemnation from her.

In the early days of my Christian walk, I wouldn't read a book without telling Vivian about it to make sure that everything in it was sound. She and her husband, Sid, introduced Larry and me to the Ben Lippen Christian Life Conferences in Asheville, North Carolina. These conferences had a big impact on Larry and me.

Vivian was a gift from God to me because she was the one who helped me become established in God's truth. There are no words to describe how much I loved her and what she meant to me.

I soon became involved in a local women's Bible study group called Women to Women. That also played a role in my walk with the Lord. Martha Linderholm was our Bible teacher, and she faithfully taught us biblical truths each week. She was an amazing lady who loved the Lord and was faithful in teaching us week after week, year after year. It was wonderful how I would hear a truth from Vivian and then go to my Bible study with Martha and hear the same truth.

God used my involvement with Women to Women in many ways during my growth as a believer. Later, I was asked to serve on the Women to Women board, which I did for about twenty-five years. We not only had weekly Bible studies taught by Martha, but also yearly retreats. These retreats provided sound biblical teaching as well as wonderful fellowship. They played a major role in my life as well as the lives of many others.

Another example of God's grace in helping me grow as a new believer was learning more about the sovereignty of God. My first realization of this truth was within the first two or three years after I was saved.

I was sitting in my bedroom, reading Psalm 139. As I read, I would stop and meditate on what it said and think about what it meant in my life. How would I live differently and respond to the circumstances in my life if I really believed this? The more I read that psalm and pondered what it was saying, the more I realized that God knew everything. The psalm tells how God watched me being formed in my mother's womb and knew all the days that were ordained for me. It also talks about how God knows every thought we ever think and every word we will ever say.

The truth of God's sovereignty and what all that meant began to come alive to me. I remember thinking, *Lord, You knew all about me. You saw me like an ultrasound.* (Have you ever thought that God saw us in the womb long before man ever invented the ultrasound?) I realized if God saw that, He knew about everything that touched my life.

When this truth began to really sink in, it was hard for me to understand that God loved me; yet He knew that Dad's death twenty-four hours after my car wreck would have such a devastating effect on my life. I thought, *God, You could have kept that from happening, and You didn't; yet I know You love me. Why did You allow this to happen if You really love me?*

I began to look at my past in light of other truths I knew about God: that He is all-knowing and all-seeing and that He's a God of love, mercy, and grace. The truth of the sovereignty of God began to really grab hold of my heart. Romans 8:28 says, "And we know that in all things God works for the good of those who love Him, who have been called according to His purpose." That verse says "we know that in all things." I began to focus on the words *know* and *all* in that verse. I asked God to help me understand and apply the truths He was teaching me.

I first settled in my heart the truth of who God is and what He says about Himself. Then I decided that God was God and that I would believe and trust Him to be *all* that He says He is—even though I didn't understand why He allowed certain things to happen. I knew I must settle forever who God is and that I would never know who God is until I knew the truth of His Word. In John 17:17, Jesus said, "Sanctify them by the truth; your Word is truth." The more I studied my Bible, the more I understood.

The story of Joseph in Genesis 37–50 really helped me. Many things—bad things—happened to Joseph. His brothers treated him terribly; yet he made some astounding statements in Genesis 45:1–8. Over and over, he said it was God who sent him there; yet as you read the story, you know it was his brothers who sold him into slavery. Genesis 50:19–20 says, "Joseph said to them, 'Don't be afraid. Am I in the place of God? You intended to harm me, but God intended it for good to accomplish what is now being done, the saving of many lives.'"

As I read these verses, I thought, *God, how could Joseph respond to his brothers like that?* I knew I wouldn't have responded so nicely. I would have wanted to make them suffer for all the heartache they had caused me. So I asked Him, "God, what did Joseph know about You that would cause him to respond that way? I want to know You like that."

From then on, when I read passages like Abraham offering Isaac, David facing Goliath, and all the heroes of the Bible, I would ask, "Lord, what did they know about You that I don't know, and will You teach me what they knew about You? I want to be like that. Lord, you said David was a man after your own heart; I want to be a woman after your own heart. Please do that work of grace in me."

As I continued studying God's Word, it was evident these men in the Bible trusted God's character and His Word. They lived their lives believing that God is who He says He is—a faithful God who keeps His promises. Numbers 23:19 says, "God is not a man, that He should lie, nor a son of man, that He should change His mind. Does He speak and then not act? Does He promise and not fulfill?" The more I learned about God through His Word and promises, the more I began to rest in these promises and look at the circumstances of my life, knowing that God was and is in control. I began to respond differently to people as well as my circumstances, applying the truths I was learning. I trusted that He works *all* things—the good, bad, insignificant, things I think are so important, disappointing things, and happy things—and He works them together for our good and His glory.

I asked myself these questions: *What if I really believed these truths in His Word? How would my life be different? Would I respond differently to people and my circumstances?* I was soon to learn the answers to these questions as I put into practice what God was teaching me.

God began dealing with me about my relationship with my mother. Her years of alcoholism and behavior toward me had destroyed any love I felt for her. I never trusted her with my children. For example, when Larry and I were in the Air Force, he was out of the country for four months, and I flew back to my hometown to stay with Larry's mom and dad, whom I called Mom and Pop. At the time, Fran was two weeks old, and Debbie was twenty-three months.

I knew I needed help with the children, and I could not depend on my mother. I did not want to put my children and myself back in that environment with her alcoholism. It was an awkward situation, but I had to think of my children. Our children were the only grandchildren that Mom and Pop had, and Mother had seventeen. I was very close to them, especially Mom, and they were wonderful to the girls and me. I had almost no relationship with my own mother.

I was forty-one years old when God began to reconnect us. Mother was diagnosed with cancer that had metastasized. I knew God was telling me to go and help take care of her. I absolutely did not want to go. Again, I was reading Psalm 139 and sensed the Lord saying to me, "Grace, you've got to take this as coming from Me. You don't understand, but you have got to trust Me with this. I know how you feel toward your mother, but I love her, and she does not know Me. Will you go and let Me love your mother through you?"

I knew what God wanted me to do. I knew He was asking me to trust Him—that He loved me and that nothing touched my life that did not first come through His hand and heart of love. Peace came over me, and I realized that but for the grace of God in my life,

I could have allowed drinking to control my life to the extent that she did. I could have responded to circumstances just as she did. I'm capable of doing anything anyone else does. If it weren't for God's grace, where would any of us be? My mother did not know the Lord, and now God was saying to me, "I want you to go and minister to your mother. I love you, and I am with you."

If God had not taught me what He did in Psalm 139, I couldn't have done it. This was an act of obedience. I could see God's hand at work in my life. I had learned obedience from my earthly father, and I knew I needed to obey and do what God said. I needed to obey not out of fear of punishment, but out of my love for Him.

As I drove the car to see Mother, I was sobbing all the way, telling the Lord, "I dislike her and can't stand for her to touch me, and I don't want to go." In the beginning, every time I would be around her, these horrible memories came flooding back. I would say to the Lord, "You are sending me there, and You live in me, and there is nowhere I go that You are not there. I know from Your word (Hebrews 13:20–21) that You never call me to do anything that You don't equip me to do, so I am going to bodily take myself there, but if anything is going to happen, You will have to do it because I can't."

Again, I went back to the things I knew to be true about God. I knew that there was nowhere I went where He was not with me because God promises in Hebrews 13:5b that He will never leave or forsake me. I trusted in these truths from God's Word and went to help Mother, knowing that God would do a work in my heart to minister to her—and He did. I knew He would be faithful and put that desire in my heart to help her. As John 10:4 says, He also promises that where He sends forth His sheep, He goes before them. True to Himself, God did go ahead of me and equip me, and He even prepared my mother's heart.

I would walk in her house, praying "God, You love her, so please, You are going to have to fill me with a love for her because I don't have it." In the beginning, I was there only in obedience, but God began to change my heart. Over time, God gave me an incredible love for my mother—to the point that I just wanted to hold her. It had been many years since I could stand to touch her or have her touch me. It was wonderful to see and experience this enormous change in my life.

I took her to the doctor for chemo treatments, did her grocery shopping, and tried to cook food that she could eat and enjoy. Mother saw this big change in me and said, "Grace, you're different." I told her it was because of the Lord and what He had done in my life. She said to me, "Now honey, it's okay to be religious, but you don't want to become a religious fanatic. That would be foolish."

Everything in me wanted to say to her, "I would not even be here at all if God had not sent me," but I didn't because I knew I shouldn't and that it would hurt her. Instead, I just looked at her and said, "Mother, if you only knew what the Lord Jesus Christ has done for me. I'd be a fool for Him anywhere, any time."

Eventually, when she would let me, I would share with her my testimony and what God had done in my life. We both began to look forward to my weekly visits. I normally went on Monday and returned home on Wednesday morning. God changed both of us, and it reached the point that as soon as I arrived, she would say, "Honey, so-and-so said, 'Next time Grace comes, please call me.'" So Mother would call the person, and when they came over, she would say to me, "Tell them what you have told me." I started sharing my testimony with her friends. I continued praying for Mother to trust Christ as her Savior.

One day in the summer of 1979, while Larry and I were at a Ben Lippen Bible Conference in Asheville, North Carolina, I received a message to call Mother. Because I knew how sick she had been, I was concerned when I received the message that she had called. She told me she wanted me to be the first to know what she had done. She had been thinking about all that I had shared with her about the Lord and that Anne had come by the house and talked with her. She said that she had prayed and trusted Christ as her Savior and wanted me to know. Words cannot describe how happy I was.

What God taught me through this time and how He worked in my heart brought about one of my greatest growth periods as a believer. I went in obedience to the Lord, and He did an amazing work of grace in my heart.

Harder than overcoming my bitterness toward my mother was overcoming my fear of speaking in public. God began working on me in this area almost immediately.

When I was saved in April 1976, the one thing I asked the Lord was to please not ever ask me to speak in front of people—not even two or three. But He had other plans for me. The Lord was very loving toward me and dealt with me in small steps. I think it was the very next day after I became a Christian that I got a call from a lady in the church inviting me to a prayer meeting or something, and I was petrified. Up until this point, I didn't go anywhere that I might be called on to pray or read. This fear had controlled me as long as I can remember. It ruled my life and affected many decisions I made. Larry was the only person who knew how bad it was.

This fear was so terrible that I wouldn't attend Sunday school or any other function where I thought they might go around the room and ask participants to tell their names. I would do anything to avoid something like that. I know that sounds absolutely crazy, but I had become more and more in bondage to this fear. Before I became a Christian, I would freely have gone to a party where there was drinking or to someone's house to play bridge, but never somewhere I might be called upon to speak, pray, or read something.

When this phone call came for me to go to this prayer thing, I was really scared. But I had given my life to Christ, and I had determined on that day in April, He was Lord of my life. Whatever He told me to do, even if it killed me, I was going to do it. So the next day, with fear and trembling, I went to this prayer thing, and sure enough, they handed me a piece of paper with a name on it and asked me to pray for that person. All I said was, "I pray for so-and-so. Amen." That was my first small step of faith.

Not long after that, my sister, Anne, called and asked if I would come share my testimony with her Sunday school class. Again, I was scared to death! But I wanted more than anything to be obedient to the Lord, so I went. I thought I was going to be talking to maybe ten to fifteen people, but there was a roomful! I was very afraid, and there was a voice saying, "You can't do this! Run! Run!" Only God held me in that seat. I remember standing up and clutching my Bible. I cannot tell you anything I said, but I tried to relate to the people what God had done in my life.

This was a gradual process, and God did test my faith. In those first few years, He called me to do the very thing I feared the most. Only God knows the depth of fear I had and what it took for me to go to the places He was calling me to speak. Every time I stepped out in faith to whatever God called me to do, God showed Himself to be faithful. That's really how God has worked in me. He's been very gentle and loving. He kept reminding me (especially in the beginning), "Grace, I know your frame. Remember, I watched you being formed in your mother's womb (Psalm 139:14–16). I know why you're so fearful, and I want to deliver you from this bondage." And bondage it was.

I had already seen how God delivered me from the bondage of alcohol, prescription drugs, and cigarettes. God did that instantly with me. Now He began to take away the fears that had held me in bondage for so many years. God was teaching me to walk by faith and not by sight (Galatians 3:11) and trust in His love, faithfulness, and promises. I was slowly learning to live my life by faith alone.

God continued to deal with me about my fear of speaking. In the summer of 1979, while Larry and I were at a Ben Lippen conference, we sang the hymn "Take My Life and Let it Be." The speaker asked while we were singing that if God spoke to us in any way, would we simply stand up and then sit right back down to acknowledge to the Lord that we were responding. When it came to the line "take my voice," I thought I was going to have a heart attack because my heart was beating so fast. I knew exactly what that meant. God was saying, "Grace, trust me with your voice." I knew in my heart that God was calling me to be a Bible teacher, so I immediately stood up and sat back down.

Two days later, when we were back home in Columbia, one of the ministers from church came to me while I was working in the nursery and said, "Grace, we think the Lord is calling you to teach, and we want you to start a college class." Because of my fear, I had hidden out for years by working in the church nursery rather than going to a Sunday school class. Out of obedience to the Lord, I soon started the class.

The first Sunday, a young college student who was like a son to me was the only person to come. I was scared just talking to him! Then much to my horror, halfway through the lesson, another young man came in, and I spent the rest of the hour trying to convince him he should go to the career class because he worked and went to college. (I was trying to get him out of mine!) He was very polite and said, "Yes, Ma'am" but would not leave the class. Much to my chagrin, the next Sunday, he was back, along with another person, so I now had three people in my class. I spent a good part of the class still trying to convince the same boy that he needed to attend the career class. Again, he was very polite but wouldn't leave my class.

The church leadership provided me with a list of names of college kids who had quit coming to church so I could call them and invite them to the class. I would faithfully call, tell them about the class, and then hang up the phone and pray that they wouldn't come because I was so afraid! Thank goodness the Lord didn't listen to me. The next Sunday, I had three more come, but I was shaking so badly that I could hardly talk. I was very glad I was sitting down because my legs were trembling, so there was no way that they would have supported me standing up.

I looked at those students and said I needed to pray because there was no way I could do this, and if God wanted it done, He would have to do it. The class said to me, "You know, you said you couldn't do this, but we didn't believe you, and now we know you really can't, so we will pray for you." And these few students started praying for me to be able to talk so I could teach them.

That incident was the best thing that could have happened to the class and me. God used it to draw us to one another. The class realized that I must really love and care about them to put myself through the agony of trying to teach, and it endeared us to each other. We became a team pulling for one another. I had a student tell me he had to give a speech at the local university, and he was very afraid. He said he thought about my fear and thought, *if Mrs. Hamrick can do it, so can I.*

I continued teaching that class for two years, and as I made calls and invited students to my class, I told them my story about how I would not go to Sunday school because of my fear of reading or praying. I promised them if they came to the class, they had my word that I would never call on them to say a word or pray if they didn't want to. These young college students, some who hadn't been in Sunday school for years, started coming, and the class grew.

I remember another time when my faith was really being stretched. I had been saved maybe four years at this point, and several speaking opportunities were given to me. I was afraid and overwhelmed. One afternoon, I was crying out to God because I wanted to obey Him; yet I was still very afraid. That Wednesday night, I was at church, and my pastor, W. L. Collins, was talking about how God led the children of Israel out of Egypt and how their shoes never wore out. He told how God lovingly and gently led them out of Egypt and into the wilderness and took care of them for forty years.

It was like God just spoke to my heart and said, "Grace, don't you know that I know you, and I understand your fear? I love you, and I am not going to put you in a place where I will not be there to equip you to do whatever I call you to do. I am not going to overwhelm you. See how gently I led the children of Israel—and I am the same God. I am gently leading you. Will you trust Me?"

After the service was over, I was crying because it moved me how God had clearly spoken to my heart. I walked up to my pastor, who had been with the church for a couple of years and had never seen anything but a big smile on my face. I think it scared him to see me crying. I told him I wanted to talk with him, and he asked me to come to his office and tell him what was wrong. When I told him about all the public speaking and my terrible fear, he had to fight to keep from laughing because he thought something really horrible had happened to me. He was relieved to hear that was all it was.

I looked at him and said, "You don't understand. No one but God understands the intense fear I have." I told him, to let him have some idea how fearful I was, "If God told me to stand in front of a firing squad and let people shoot bullets at me and trust Him that one second before that bullet would hit my body, God would stick out His hand and stop the bullet, or if God would say, 'Grace, I want you to stand on the top of the roof of this building, and there is going to be an invisible sidewalk, and you step on it' or 'Grace, you get up and speak in front of ten people,' I would take the top of the building or the firing squad any day." I was petrified. I know this is hard for anyone who does not have this consuming fear to understand. I think my pastor began to understand the depth of my fear. He prayed for me and encouraged me to trust the Lord.

I realized again that God knew me. He understood all my past, had given me the personality I had, and loved me. I knew that as a mother or father gently leads a child, I could trust God to lead me to victory with this fear. I determined again that whatever God asked me to do, I would do it, believing and trusting His deliverance. That's when the journey of speaking and teaching really began. I can say that God has never failed to equip me to do it. When I was shaking to pieces right before I stood up to speak somewhere, God always calmed me down.

For years, I prayed, "Lord, You deliver me the moment that I stand up to teach; why don't You deliver me from this permanently so I won't be dying a thousand deaths before I have to speak?"

It was like the Lord spoke to my heart and said, "Grace, if I did that, you would not need Me. You wouldn't be as dependent on Me."

I realized that was true, so I began to pray, "Lord, don't ever take it away from me, because I want to always be dependent on You to do the impossible through me."

I am not saying that it worked instantly for me to be able to go and stand up to teach. I taught in Sunday school for seven or eight years sitting down before I could stand up and teach because my legs would shake so badly. But God has been faithful to me all these years and brought me through each and every time I taught. This was just the beginning of my learning that God is a loving and faithful God who equips you to do anything He calls you to do (Hebrews 13: 20–21).

Not only did God transform my fear into faith, but He also transformed Larry's and my marriage, making it more wonderful than before. As Larry and I began to study God's Word, go to conferences like the Ben Lippen conference, listen to sound biblical teaching, and grow in the Lord, our marriage changed drastically. It was wonderful, and we loved each other in a deeper way. Did we ever fuss again? Yes, but we were quicker to apologize and ask for forgiveness.

I was bad about arguing and fussing with Larry. One of the first verses that I read after I began my Christian walk was Philippians 2:14: "Do everything without complaining or arguing." I knew that was for me—it was like the words jumped off the page when I read them. I asked the Lord to please change me and help me be the wife Larry needed. And God began to really change me.

One day, I was busy doing something, and Larry asked me to run some errands for him. I had a lot going on, and the last thing I wanted was to stop and run errands for him. I told him I was busy and couldn't do it. Quickly, the Lord began to deal with me about my attitude. I kept telling myself what I was doing was just as important as what he was doing and that he could do it himself. But God was changing my heart, and I decided I would go and do the errands he asked and trust God to help me finish what I thought was so important to me. Amazingly, I did all the errands Larry asked me to do and everything I wanted to do. It went quickly, and everything worked out just great.

It was in little steps that God continued to change me. I was learning that I could either do things His way or mine, and His way was always the best. Daily, in the big and small choices, I wanted to apply what God was teaching me in His Word. I discovered it was really a heart issue. Was it going to be my way or God's? When I lived my life applying God's truth in my decisions and marriage, things always seemed to turn out right. I learned God blesses us when we obey Him. Larry and I saw the difference it was making in our marriage and home.

I liked what God was doing in me and how He was putting a different desire in me. It had a big impact on Larry. I would often hear him say to someone, "Grace's life has been such a witness to me as I have watched her trust and obey the Lord."

God began to change both of us. Often I prayed, "God, change Larry." But it was *me* God wanted to change. He changed Larry too, but I knew He wanted to change me.

We started praying together and began to work as a team. There is a huge difference between a marriage without Christ as head of the home and a marriage with Christ as head of that home. We often taught that if you treat your wife as God commands you to, the wife feels like a queen who is loved and respected. And if the wife treats the husband as God commands, he is honored and respected. It really makes a big difference in a home and marriage. We knew what a marriage was like for twenty years without this, and we learned the last thirty years of our marriage how wonderful a godly marriage can be if we will trust and obey God. When we honor God, He honors us.

Larry and I both felt like Paul, who said, "Christ Jesus came into the world to save sinners, of whom I am the worst." (1 Timothy 1:15). But thanks be to God, He can change lives for His glory.

I am very thankful that the Lord gave me such a love for His Word and the ability to call it into remembrance. I know He is sanctifying me through His Word. He is sanctifying us as He brings people, circumstances, and many other things into our lives. It is our response to what the Lord has allowed to touch our lives that either delights His heart or grieves Him. We cannot choose what comes across our paths or what happens to us, but we can choose to believe and trust God in and through it. This is why it is so important to settle forever the truth that God loves you and demonstrated His love for you on the cross. He died for you so that you may be with Him for all eternity.

The Bible is God's special love letter to you. Learning to act upon the truths I knew about God was a big step in my sanctification process. He has always been faithful to me and true to His Word.

CHAPTER 6

Sharing Grace

> I hear about your faith in the Lord Jesus and your
> love for all the saints. I pray that you may be active
> in sharing your faith, so that you will have a full
> understanding of every good thing we have in Christ.
> —Philemon 1:5–6

> He will my shield and portion be as long as life endures.
> —John Newton

My journey had begun, and I never could have imagined what my future held. I knew I wanted to share with others what the Lord had done in my life. He had showered me with His grace, and I wanted Him to bring people in my life so I could tell them about Him. I prayed that He would do that for me.

My heart's desire was to know God, learn more about His Word, and listen for and obey His voice, even when I thought it seemed inconsequential to me. For example, the Lord may prompt me to call or pray for someone. It may be a little thing, but knowing that God is telling me to do it makes me want to obey. I want to sense that nudging from the Lord and obey in faith without giving it a second thought—even though I don't know what may be ahead.

One such incident happened within the first year I was saved. There was a couple whom I will call Suzy and Jim. They were stationed at the Army base, Fort Jackson, in Columbia, South Carolina. At our Wednesday night prayer meeting, they shared that they had been praying for God to send someone to keep their children while Suzy, who was pregnant with their third child, had her baby. Since their families were not close by and they didn't have the finances to hire help, this was a huge need. Because prayer requests were given at the beginning of the service, by the time the service was over, I had forgotten the request.

A few days later, the Lord reminded Larry and me of this need. The next Sunday, I told Jim we would like to keep the children when the baby came. After church, I met Suzy and found out the baby was due in a few weeks. I told her that would give us plenty of time for the children and me to become better acquainted before the baby arrived.

Suzy and I made plans for me to come to her house the following week, but at 7:15 the next morning, Jim was at our door. He didn't just have his two children, but four, all under the age of five. Two of them were his, and the other two were foster children they had previously taken in. So much for our long-range plans of getting acquainted before the baby arrived!

I was taking care of three young girls and a little boy, plus a Bible study was going to take place at my house in just a couple of hours. I cried out, "Lord, what am I going to do? *Help!*" I found a children's video and put it on, and they watched it while we had Bible study. They were very good. This was the beginning of my involvement with this family.

The first six or seven months of the baby's life, I took care of him quite frequently because Suzy had to go back into the hospital for surgery. At this point, we did not have any grandchildren, so these children became very special to us. Every Wednesday, I took Suzy and the children to our Women to Women Bible study that had a nursery. (By this time, the foster children had been placed elsewhere.) Afterward,

I would keep the three children to give her a break, and that evening, I would take them to church, and Jim would pick them up.

Larry and I became very close to this young couple. We even planned a birthday party for Jim at our house. The Wednesday night before his birthday, I was in the nursery at church when Jim came to pick up the kids. He walked in the door with a friend and said, "I want you to meet a good friend of mine. His name is Jeff Leavitt." Jeff was around nineteen years old, and I liked him instantly. I suggested he bring Jeff to our home for the party. That was the beginning of our relationship with him. Little did I know then that this young man would become such a big part of our family.

Jim and Suzy eventually moved away, but Jeff remained stationed at Ft. Jackson. He often came to our house and hung out with us. I invited him to church, and though he never wanted to go, I still invited him to Sunday dinner after church.

Jeff spent a lot of time with our family and soon came to know the Lord. But the day came when the U.S. Army assigned him to the White House to work in communications. This was during President Carter's administration, and he stayed on with President Reagan. Jeff left our home the morning of May 27, 1979, and we were not sure we would ever see him again. He was from upstate New York, and there was no reason to ever return to South Carolina. But we kept in touch, prayed for him, and remained very close.

After some time, Jeff called and said he wanted to come for a visit. Since our two oldest daughters were out of the home, we had a couple of spare bedrooms. Jeff liked one bedroom in particular and called it his own.

During his visit, I said to him, "You have traveled with the President to different parts of the world. Tell me, what is the most wonderful place you've been?"

Jeff just stood, looking out the window in our den, and I thought he was never going to answer me. He turned and looked at me with tears in his eyes and said, "I've found something here that I haven't found anywhere else." What he said touched me deeply. He had left here a new Christian and felt much love and support as a new believer from the church and us. I knew he missed us terribly, but I had not realized how much. Jeff's visit was the beginning of something new God was doing in Jeff's life and in ours.

During those five years that Jeff was assigned to the White House, Larry and I prayed for a Christian wife for him. And I can tell you, God answered our prayers. Many times, he would be dating a girl, and we would pray, "Lord, if she isn't the one for Jeff, please don't let them marry."

In the meantime, God brought a beautiful young lady into our lives. Her name was Dionne, and we became very close. We often met together to pray. She later moved away from Columbia but often came and spent the weekend with us. She'd call and say, "Is my bedroom ready?" And of course, we'd say yes. Dionne would come and spend the weekend with us in our guest bedroom (which Jeff called his). This went on for a couple of years. Dionne was fast becoming like a daughter to us and was a good friend of our three daughters.

One day, Jeff called me from Washington and asked, "Is my room ready? I want to come spend the weekend." I told him of course; his room was always ready for him. He told me it would be about three more weeks and gave me the date.

A week or so later, Dionne called and said, "I've got this weekend open, and I would like to visit. Is my room ready?"

I asked, "Well, honey, you know Jeff?"

She responded, "Yes, you talk about him *all* the time."

I told her, "Well, Jeff called, and he's coming that weekend."

She jokingly said, "Well, he's not getting my room!"

"I'm sorry honey," I told her, "but he called and asked for it first, and he calls it his room too, so you'll have to sleep in the other bedroom this time."

She responded, "Well, he may get it this time, but he'll never get it again."

We both had a good laugh over that. Little did either of us know what was about to take place.

Later, Jeff called, and I told him Dionne was also coming for the weekend. I suggested he call her because she had been a little down, and I thought it might cheer her up. (Of course, the truth of the matter was that I was trying to play Cupid.)

He said, "She doesn't know who I am."

I asked, "Do you know who she is?"

"Yes, you talk about her *all* the time," he said.

"Well," I said, "Guess what? I talk to her about you *all* the time, so she will know who you are."

He did call her, and that was the beginning. That weekend, they met at our home. They weren't in the house twenty-four hours when I looked at Larry and said, "Honey, I think our children are falling in love." The Lord was answering our prayers.

Larry and I had always seen great potential in Jeff and wanted him to go to college. Within the year, Jeff came back to Columbia after his five-year assignment to the White House was completed. He decided to go to the University of South Carolina to get his degree in engineering. He lived with us for a while and then moved into an apartment. I have a picture in my den of Jeff shaking hands with President Reagan as he told him he was leaving to go back to school. In the meantime, Dionne moved back to Columbia.

Jeff finished in three years, and he and Dionne set the wedding date. His father was no longer living, but his mother, grandmother, sisters, and two of his brothers came and stayed with us for the wedding.

We also knew Dionne's mom and dad and felt very close to them. Even though it is customary for the bride's mother to sit on one side of the aisle with the groom's mother on the other, we three mothers decided to sit together in the middle of the pew, holding hands as we watched our children marry in March 1986. Years later, they had a son, Jacob, who is our eleventh grandchild.

Through these many years, they have been a huge blessing to me and the rest of the family. They are truly like our children. We all still vacation together every year and see each other during Christmas holidays.

None of this would have happened if we had not listened and responded to this nudging from the Lord about keeping Jim and

Suzy's children. I sometimes wonder how many blessings I have missed by not listening to that still, small voice. I am very thankful I listened that time.

Jeff and Dionne are not the only adopted children God has brought into our lives. Several years later, in 1982, we met Beverly and Eric Patterson when they had been married just a short time. They soon became good friends with our children, and later she and Eric were in the young married class that Larry and I taught. Over the years, the Lord knit our hearts together, and in many ways, Beverly acted more like me than any of my children. We would often joke that she really was my daughter and that they had mixed up the babies in the hospital. Of course, this was not true, but because we acted and thought so much alike, we would laugh and say it was.

Larry and I were a part of their lives before their first child, Brooke, was born. A couple of years later, Sarah was born, followed by their twins, Blake and Chad. I felt very blessed that the Lord would allow all of them to be such a part of our lives. We were Grammy and Granddaddy to their four children and were in their lives almost daily until they moved out of town.

I discipled Beverly weekly for many years after the twins were born. Titus 2 says the older women are to teach the younger women. That is what Vivian did for me, what I did for Beverly, and now what she is doing in the lives of younger women. I love when I see women whom I have discipled in turn discipling other women.

For years, after I taught a college class, Larry and I taught a class for young married couples in our church. By this time, our daughter Fran had married Allen Wise (1979), and Sandra had married Stephen Snipes (1984). Debbie, Allen, Fran, Stephen, Sandra, Jeff, Dionne, Eric, and Beverly were all in our class along with many others. We felt like we had many children in the Lord and were very blessed. We felt joyful and privileged that God called us to teach His Word not only to our children, but also to others. I felt like He gave us a second chance. Although Larry and I were not walking with the Lord when we raised our daughters, God allowed us this opportunity to not only pour truth into their lives and teach them God's Word, but also later to the next generation, as God gave four sons to Allen and Fran (Bradley, Nathan, Benjamin and Joseph) as well as a son and three daughters to Stephen and Sandra (Joshua, Kathryn, Sydney and Rachel). He graciously restored to me "the years the locust had eaten" Joel 2:25b.

God has allowed me to disciple women over the years who have in turn discipled other women. This has been an inexpressible joy to me—to see the ripple effect of His grace. Through the years, Larry would disciple the young men, and often we would meet with couples as we shared truth from God's Word. The Lord was gracious to us in many ways while we taught that class. It was a special gift for Larry and me to be able to teach all of our children, including the Leavitts and the Pattersons, God's Word.

As our family grew in many unexpected ways, another amazing thing happened. Only the Lord could have done something like this because they did not plan it—it just happened. Over a period of just a few years, all of the children—except for Jeff and Dionne, who were now living in the Washington/Baltimore area—moved onto the same street, just houses apart, in a small neighborhood that was only one mile from Larry and me. Together, there were four families that included twelve grandchildren. These children grew up like sisters and brothers, as they played together every day. All of these grandchildren were homeschooled, and because Larry and I were only one mile away, we were very involved in their lives. I often kept the younger children while their parents taught the older ones.

Larry had bought me a big van so I could take all of the grandchildren on field trips. One time, I took six of them to the mall to the Dollar Tree (which is a good deal for grandmothers). The youngest was two and the oldest seven. I put them in a straight line with Brooke, who was six, at the front of the line holding one handle of the rope. Then I took the other handle and ran the jump rope through the loop on each of their jeans and put Bradley, who was seven years old, at the back of the line, holding the other handle. This kept us all together, and I didn't have to worry about a child wandering off. We made our way into the Dollar Tree, and after everyone purchased his or her prize for the day, I left having spent $6.00 plus tax. That was a fun day, and they were very good.

I don't know what Beverly, Fran, and Sandra would have done if they had not had Debbie come over many nights after work to help feed and bathe the small children. This was especially true when we had three babies born in one week. One week after Beverly's twins were born, Fran gave birth to Benjamin. Debbie and I slept in the den that first few nights, helping Beverly with the twins. I painted Blake's big toe with nail polish when we cut the hospital armbands off so we could tell them apart.

It was wonderful living so close to the grandchildren and being a part of their lives. I would take them on field trips to the zoo, museum, and library. One day, we rode the city bus just to see what it was like. Once a year, Larry and I would take them on what we called grandchildren trips or "grand trips". We started with short trips when they were young, and as they grew older, we took trips to see the Atlanta Braves; Washington, DC; Williamsburg, Virginia; and Hershey, Pennsylvania.

We had only two rules on our trips. The number-one rule was that you had to have fun, and the second was that you had to stick close to Grammy and Granddaddy. They loved going to Myrtle Beach when they were young, and at midnight, we would take them to buy Krispy Kreme doughnuts after playing miniature golf.

I often had Bible studies along with manners school and cooking lessons in my home. They all thought that was great fun. As we studied the Bible, especially the story of Daniel, I would tell them that I wanted them to always dare to be Daniels. In Daniel 1, Daniel tells us that he "resolved not to defile himself" but chose God's way and not man's. I wanted them, even while they were still young, to always choose God's way, even though it meant standing alone. Those years of manners school and Bible study were very special, and the grandchildren seemed to love it. Years later, I had another Grammy school with my three younger grandchildren, Sydney, Joseph and Rachel, and three very close family friends, Corey, Logan, and Clay. Those were priceless times together.

We were all grateful for the time the Lord allowed us to be together. We were very involved with our grown children and grandchildren and got along amazingly. It was evident the Lord placed us together and gave us a great love for one another. We all grew in our walks with the Lord—trusting Him to lead and guide us.

Our journeys in life have many turns and detours, and the summer of 1994 was a major turn for Larry and me. Because of Larry's business, he traveled quite a lot. On this particular day, he was out of town when I received a phone call from a total stranger. This male voice identified himself as Alex, and said he was calling because he felt the Lord leading him to call my husband and me. He certainly had my attention, as he then explained to me about a recent mission trip he had taken and a man he had met on the plane. This man was a friend of ours and was well aware of our ministry with young couples.

As the two of them talked on that long trip overseas, they began to share about their ministries and needs. Alex told of his church in Columbia, which was a new church. Their problem was that it was full of young couples with lots of children, but there were no older couples in the church. Years earlier, some Clemson graduates who had been involved in Campus Crusade had moved to Columbia to start a church that they named Riverbend Community Church. The leaders had been praying for several years for the Lord to send an older couple who had a heart for young couples to come to Riverbend. Our friend on the plane told Alex about Larry and me and that for years, we had been ministering to young couples. He had felt for some time that the Lord was probably leading us out of the church we were in and to give us a call.

The day he called, he was very careful in saying he was not trying to get us to leave our church, but if at any time in the future we sensed the Lord leading us into another ministry, would we consider visiting Riverbend. I thanked him for calling and told him I would tell my husband what he had said but that we had a ministry at our church and would not leave unless the Lord made it very clear to us. He was very gracious and said he would pray for us.

The interesting part was that for many months before Alex called, Larry and I had already sensed the Lord was about to do something different with our ministry. It wasn't long—maybe two or three months—before God began to make it clear to us that He was leading us elsewhere.

Larry and I visited Riverbend that August or early September, but it was a while before we were convinced this was where God was sending us. We were teachers, and they did not have Bible classes for adults on Sunday morning. They met upstairs over a business, and there was not much room for classes. We thought this could not be where the Lord was sending us. So we started visiting other churches. But the Lord never gave us peace about any other church, so we went back to Riverbend.

It was not easy. I cried a great deal over leaving the church that had been so much a part of our lives. One day, I was reading Isaiah 43:18–19: "Forget the former things, do not dwell on the past. See, I am doing a new thing! Now it springs up; do you not perceive it? I am making a way in the desert and streams in the wasteland." As I was reading and pondering the words, they seemed to grab hold of my heart, as if God was saying to me, "Grace, trust Me, and move on. I am doing something new in your life." That was a turning point for me. Larry had already moved on, but I'm slow. Changes are not easy for me, but the Lord made it very clear this was where He wanted us at this time.

Other big life changes were on the way. After many years living in the same neighborhood, Eric and Beverly moved to another city. Several years after they left, our three daughters and their families decided it was time for them to move, too. They had all put off moving into a larger home because they enjoyed being together, but they knew the time had come for them to move.

They looked around the Columbia area to move. They were not trying to stay together; in fact, each family was looking in different areas to buy a home. As it happened, every time one of them tried to buy a house, for some reason or another, the deal fell through. This happened numerous times over a period of a couple of years.

After all of these frustrating experiences, they decided to start looking for land in a rural area. They found some land and decided they would buy it together and build their homes. The children encouraged us to sell our home and come build as well. We thanked them but declined. We told them to go with our blessing, but having been in our home for forty years, we felt we were too old to move and should stay put. We did promise to pray about it, though. As we prayed and asked others to pray with us, the Lord began to make it very clear to us that we should move onto the land with them.

God was very gracious in how He led us in our decision to move and worked out all the details. We were amazed. Two years before this, a couple who was in our Sunday school class and had been in our home many times for Bible study came up to us at a ball game and asked, "If you ever decide to sell your home, will you let us know?" We told them we had no intention of moving and couldn't imagine we would ever sell, but if we did, we would let them know.

As we began praying about the decision to move, we remembered what they had requested and gave them a call. We weren't sure they would still be interested, but when we called, they said they wanted to buy our home. This was just one of the many ways the Lord began to confirm to us that we should move. Isaiah 48:17 says, "This is what the Lord says—your Redeemer, the Holy One of Israel: I am the Lord your God, who teaches you what is best for you, who directs you in the way you should go."

We had no idea what was ahead for us, but He knew, and He led us every step of the way. We were going to learn in a deeper way the sufficiency of God's grace.

CHAPTER 7

Sufficient Grace

> My grace is sufficient for you, for my
> power is made perfect in weakness.
> —2 Corinthians 12:9
>
> Through many dangers, toils, and
> snares, I have already come.
> —John Newton

In 2002, our children sold their homes, built, and moved onto the property that we all purchased. Within a few months after selling our home, Larry and I moved in with them while our home was being built.

This was an exciting time for us with many things going on. We were very happy to be moving and were enjoying our new surroundings, especially with all of us together on our newly purchased land. I had developed some health problems a couple of years before, but I was much better, and everything was going well. When Larry and I designed our new home, we thought it would be wise because of my problems and our age, to make our home wheelchair-friendly just in case. We did this as a precaution but were hoping there would never be a need for either of us. Life was good.

Everything seemed to be going well until I went to my doctor for my annual physical in 2003. I was surprised when the doctor called me to come back for more blood work because I felt so good. I went back for more blood work, and we watched my white blood count continue to rise.

During this time, Sandra and three of the grandchildren, Joshua, Nathan, and Kathryn, were planning on going on a mission trip to Bolivia with their church. Sandra had been having some back problems, and I knew this trip was going to be very hard and was concerned about them going. Truthfully, I was worried about my health and them going on this mission trip.

St. Andrews Evangelical Church (SAE), where all our children and grandchildren are active members, was having a mission conference. Larry and I decided to attend that Sunday morning instead of going to our church. I will never forget that day. I went to church with a burden on my heart, and as I sat listening, God began to minister to me in a very powerful way. Tears began streaming down my face; they were tears of joy, not of sadness. I sensed God's presence as He just spoke to my heart about all that was on my mind concerning the mission trip and my health. I kept wiping the tears away, and I thought my heart would burst with the joy of His tender love.

Driving home from church, Larry asked what was going on. I tried to tell him what God had impressed upon my heart. The following is what I wrote in my journal:

> Sunday, March 23: Larry and I went to SAE for the morning service. During the singing, the Lord ministered to me in such an incredible way. I don't think I have ever experienced anything in church quite like that before. I understood why Peter would say, "Let's just tabernacle here together." I heard back from the first bone marrow test, and they said they did not have a good sample, but it looked okay. My doctor kept sending me back for more blood work, and my white count kept climbing. I felt something was wrong. But this

> morning, it was like the Lord showed me that everything was going to be okay. Not that I would not get sick, but that even if I was, that it was okay. It was like a taste of what heaven must be like—I sensed His love and peace that [were] just too wonderful for words. It was the peace that passes all understanding. I felt like He was preparing me for something. I must remember that what God has shown me in the light, I must not doubt in the dark. There could be dark days ahead.

It wasn't long before we moved in our new home, and that same day, I found out I had some form of cancer. My doctor sent me to an oncologist, and after a number of tests, he felt I had some form of cancer—possibly chronic lymphocytic leukemia—and recommended I go to MD Anderson Hospital in Houston, Texas for further tests. I don't think anyone is ever prepared to hear the dreaded C-word. I felt like the rug had been yanked out beneath me. I wrote the following in my journal:

> April 20, 2003. Now it is Easter Sunday, and I now know that I do have some form of cancer and will be leaving for MD Anderson Hospital in Houston next Sunday. I am so thankful for that Sunday in March at SAE. Again, I must remember what the Lord has shown me in the light, I must not doubt in the dark. Again, I have a sense there could be dark days ahead.

We flew to Houston and stayed with our dear friends, Anne and Tom. Anne and I had been close friends since the fourth grade. Debbie flew to be with us a few days later.

That Monday, after reviewing all the tests that my doctors at home had done, they told me they wanted to do other tests to confirm their suspicion that I had mantle cell lymphoma. They talked about the possibility of us staying for six more weeks for chemotherapy if their diagnosis was correct. I knew about mantle cell lymphoma and knew the seriousness of it, so I was shocked when the doctors told me that was what they thought I had. We sat there, listening to the doctors' words, but it was like they wouldn't register in my brain. I know my response probably wasn't a normal one. I listened to what he had to say, and we asked some questions. It was as though what I was hearing was happening to someone else, not me. It was strange.

As Larry and I walked out to the waiting room where our friends, Tom and Anne, were waiting, I know I had a shocked look on my face because Anne asked, "Grace, what is it?"

We told Anne and Tom what the doctor said, and as I was telling Anne, I said to the Lord, "Lord, I don't understand." I knew the Lord had shown me that Sunday at SAE that everything would be all right. Instantly, the Lord spoke to my heart and reminded me what I had written in my journal: "What I have shown you, don't doubt now." It was very clear to me that I almost yelled, I was so excited. A big grin came on my face.

It was so noticeable to Anne that she again asked, "Grace, what is it?"

I grabbed her by the arm while steering her toward a sofa in the waiting room and said, "Anne, I don't know if I can really explain this to you, but I want to tell you what just happened." I told her about that Sunday at SAE, what the Lord had taught me then, and how He reminded me not to doubt Him now. I told her I didn't understand what all that meant, but I just knew that everything was going to be okay. We both laughed and cried, hugging each other with joy.

The doctors at the hospital said they wanted to run their own tests that week and set up the appointments for me to come back the next day. After all the tests were finally finished, I had an appointment to go back the following Monday to hear the results.

Our other two daughters, Fran and Sandra, were at home, calling daily with words of encouragement. One of the verses they said to me that gave me great comfort was Zephaniah 3:17: "The Lord your God is with you. He is mighty to save. He will take great delight in you, He will quiet you with his love, He will rejoice over you with singing."

I was comforted, but I must say, I had a rough week as I watched Larry and my loved ones grieving over what was happening to me.

The thought of having to stay another six weeks for treatment was depressing. I wanted very badly to get back with the rest of my family and our new home. Many people were praying for me, and I could feel their prayers. However, it broke my heart that my family back in Columbia was trying to deal with the bad news, and Larry and I were not there to comfort them. That was very hard on me.

The doctors recommended we start treatment as soon as the latest test results were in, and watching Larry and Debbie make plans for a long stay in Houston was tough. I did really well as long as I kept my focus on what I sensed the Lord had told me and was still showing me.

The Sunday before I went back to the hospital on Monday to hear the results was not good. I felt extremely tired and sleepy. I stayed in bed most of the day because I felt so tired. That night, in South Carolina, my pastor, elders, and many church members called a special time of prayer for me. I later found out many churches and people in different parts of the world were praying for me during this time. It was a humbling experience.

The following is part of an e-mail Sandra sent to me.

> I am praying you will really sleep tonight. Call me in the a.m.
>
> One more thought (as if that surprises you)—on this side of the journey, I can't help but think of all the people in Scripture and all the cloud of witnesses that have been called to walk a road they never would have chosen themselves. Some went kicking and screaming. Others surrendered their will to His. For some people, it turned out not as painful as they anticipated; for others, it was hard and difficult; and others—it was excruciating. But the treasures during the journey were matched perfectly to the degree of suffering. We stand now on 4/24/03 not knowing what our walk will be but understanding that ultimately, it really doesn't matter because of who we belong to! I pray that we continue to have His strength to surrender our will, that we look for His treasures, and that people won't see the deeds of man but the work of our glorious God!

"The Lord is with me, I will not be afraid. What can man do to me?" (Psalm 118:6)

"God is our refuge and strength, an ever-present help in trouble. Therefore we will not fear, though the earth give, and though the mountains fall into the heart of the sea" (Psalm 46).

Our daughter, Fran, said a missionary home on furlough told her at church that during the night, he woke up praying for me, and the Lord kept reminding him of Isaiah 41:10. She called me that Sunday afternoon to tell me. The verse says, "So do not fear, for I am with you, do not be dismayed for I am your God. I will strengthen you and help you. I will uphold you with my righteous right hand." The minute I read it, I felt like a weight had been lifted off me. I got out of bed, went downstairs, and joined Anne, Tom, Larry, and Debbie. I felt good the rest of the day.

The next morning, we all drove back to MD Anderson hospital for the results. They told me the test revealed I did *not* have mantle cell lymphoma but chronic lymphocytic leukemia. In comparison, that was wonderful news for us. I did not have to have any treatment but would have to see an oncologist on a regular basis.

We flew home the next day after being gone for over a week and discovered the children and grandchildren had unpacked our things and had our new house ready for our return. This was a wonderful surprise because we had to leave right after moving in our new home to go to Houston, and we had left with boxes still packed up all over the house.

It was a blessing and joy to get back home with all of our loved ones. We returned home on our grandson Benjamin's birthday in May 2003. The next month, Sandra, Joshua, Nathan, and Kat went on their mission trip to Bolivia. Again, the peace God had given to me that Sunday at SAE that everything would be okay was true. The Lord took them safely there and brought them safely home, just as He did for me.

The year 2004 was a busy year as we settled into our new home. Larry and I loved being there, surrounded by our children and grandchildren. He cleared an area near our home as a prayer garden and put a couple of cast iron benches for a place to sit. We have plenty of rocks here, and Larry greatly enjoyed using the rocks to make a path leading to his prayer garden as well as to create a border around our yard. We were very pleased with the results.

As far as my health, I was doing really well, and the only difference was that I had slowed down quite a bit. The children would say, "Mama, you have just slowed down enough that now we can keep up with you." All was well, and everything was going great. Larry and I were enjoying our ministry of discipling men and women. But things were soon to change.

In the summer of 2005, a lot was happening. Two of our grandsons, Nathan and Joshua (nineteen and eighteen years old), went to Indonesia on a mission trip with Dave and Esther Scovill for a month. Dave and Esther had ministered to the Dani tribe for forty years and were in the process of translating the Bible in their language.

Earlier in the year, Larry went for a physical, and they discovered he had prostate cancer. It was in the early stages, and we were very hopeful. He decided to have prostate surgery at Johns Hopkins Hospital in Baltimore. We left in August for the surgery and stayed with Jeff, Dionne, and Jacob until he was well enough to fly home. The surgery went very well, and we were especially thankful when, months later, they told us he was completely free from prostate cancer.

During this time, our oldest grandson, Bradley, had graduated from Clemson University and was preparing to go to Niger, Africa to share the good news of Jesus Christ and His love with an unreached people group in a very remote area. We knew he would be gone for at least two years. It was going to be very difficult, and even though Larry and I had prayed for our children and grandchildren to go wherever the Lord wanted them to go, a piece of my heart went with him. When Nathan and Joshua went away for a month, that was hard—but two years!

I thought, *Lord, so much is happening so fast—selling our home of forty years, building a home and moving, my cancer, Larry's cancer, and and now this—the longest separation we'd ever had from a family member so far.* I cried buckets. I don't think it would have been so hard if he had not been in such a difficult place. We prayed for his health and safety and that he would learn and be able to speak the language quickly. We prayed for the hearts of the people to be open to the gospel.

Bradley left in September, and it was about this time that Larry noticed a good bit of pain in his right leg and hip. He would laugh and say, "Honey, getting old is not for sissies." He thought it was just arthritis. But by November, it was getting worse, and his doctor ordered a lot of tests, including an MRI.

We were very busy at this time, working with two couples who were having major problems in their marriages as well as preparing to start a new Sunday morning Bible class in our church for young married couples. We were ready to get the class started and were thankful we were still able to be involved. We officially started the class on Sunday, December 11, 2005 and were very excited.

The next day, we received a phone call that you pray will never come. The reports were back, and Larry had been diagnosed with lung cancer that had metastasized. It was in his bone and liver and he only had a couple of months to live.

We were in shock. We could not believe it—he looked so good, and except for the pain in his hip and leg, he seemed to feel okay. It was very hard to take in this devastating news.

Three days later, we were in the den, watching the news before going to bed. Larry stood up to walk back to our bedroom. After taking several steps, he looked at me and said, "I can't make it."

I didn't know how I could manage to get him to bed and said, "Lord, help me. What can I do?" I immediately thought about my computer chair, which is on rollers, and was able to get him in the chair. Because we have hardwood floors, I was able to roll him in that chair to the bathroom and then to bed without difficulty. The next morning, I rolled him to the car and took him to the doctor. As I drove there, we both marveled at God's leading in our move to be near our children as well as the fact that we had built our home to be wheelchair-friendly. The doctor had a wheelchair delivered to our home that same day.

It was hard to believe that within two days of being diagnosed, Larry was dependent on a wheelchair. He had radiation treatment that took away the pain in his hip and leg. Later, he had chemotherapy. However, he never had the strength to walk again. That Christmas season, he had to go into the hospital a couple of times because his health was declining so rapidly. Because of this, we began to realize that if Larry was ever going to see Bradley again, we needed to get him home right away. He flew home from Africa on December 27 and was able to stay about ten days.

During all this time, I don't know what we would have done without our family close by, and we thanked God for leading us to move, even though we had been hesitant to do so. Everyone pitched in and helped in whatever was needed. Because the children were being home-schooled, the older grandchildren helped homeschool the younger ones as well as taking Larry to chemotherapy and radiation appointments. Without being told, the grandchildren took charge of the cooking, cleaning, yard work, etc. It was neat to watch them. They were very responsible and helpful, and it allowed us all to have quality time together.

Our extended family, close friends, and church members were a blessing as well. Occasionally, someone would spend the night here so I could get a good night's sleep, and others cleaned and ran errands. Allen and Stephen were a huge help. I tell people what wonderful sons-in-law (whom I call sons-in-love) the Lord has blessed me with. They are very good to me and do a lot for me. I always joked with Fran and Sandra and told them not to ever come to me and complain about their husbands because I would probably take their side. We were fed, prayed for, and loved in countless ways, and there is no way I could thank our loved ones enough for all they did.

After taking steroids, there were a couple of Sundays when Larry felt well enough to go to church, even though he was no longer able to walk. Our pastor asked if he had the strength and felt well enough to speak to the congregation. I pushed his wheelchair to the front of the church, and he spoke about the faithfulness of God, what He can do in a life and family, and that our foundation is in Christ alone. When we trust in Him, our foundations are firm and cannot be shaken. No matter what happens, the Lord is our shepherd. He is in us, with us, and sees us through the storms of life. And though we walk through the shadow of death, we fear no evil, for He is with us. He comforts us, and we know we will dwell in the house of the Lord forever (Psalm 23).

His health continued to decline quickly, and I was determined that as long as we could take care of him at home, we were not going to put him in the hospital. Eventually, we had a hospital bed delivered, and hospice provided the care we needed, along with our oncologist and his assistant. They helped us a great deal. By February, we knew he would not live much longer.

I had the hospital bed right beside our bed, and the night of February 17, I was in our bed with my arm across his chest when I awoke, realizing his breathing had changed. It was around 2:15 in the morning, and Sandra was spending the night with me along with a friend who was a nurse. I woke Sandra up, and we called the other family to come quickly. They were there in just minutes, and we gathered around his bed, sang "Amazing Grace," and prayed. As I watched him having difficulty breathing, I prayed for the Lord to please take him home. In just a matter of seconds, he stopped breathing. The love of my life was gone. I couldn't imagine life without him. But the Lord had been lovingly preparing me for this moment.

I was very thankful we were able to keep him home, as he was able to be around all of his family during those final weeks. Jeff, Dionne, Jacob, Beverly, Eric, Brooke, Cooper, Sarah, Chad, and Blake were there as much as they could be during those final weeks. They all came the Saturday he went home to be with the Lord.

About a month before Larry died, he was sitting in his favorite chair in the den, and I had a pillow on the floor with my head in his lap. I was crying and telling him I wanted to go with him because I didn't want to live without him. I begged the Lord to take me with him, but that was not God's plan. Even as I am writing, the tears are flowing because it is very hard to tell this. I knew I could not make it without Larry. I did not want to live without him. That day, as I was crying, he was stroking my hair, saying, "Honey, the Lord is not through with you yet. He has something else He wants you to do."

I miss him so much that it hurts. But his words keep reminding me this is true and to keep going. I have learned in a way I have never known before that God's grace is sufficient. I have never experienced such deep pain along with such incredible joy. The peace and joy of the Lord are beyond understanding. It is impossible to explain. To be understood, it must be experienced.

It wasn't until I wrote this book that I noticed the similarities (and vast differences) in two of the most painful moments of my life. The night my dad died, I sat at my mother's feet with my head in her lap, longing for comfort as I cried out, "I killed him!" There were no words of comfort, no hope—just total despair. She sat there because I'm sure she felt immense grief and hopelessness, too. Fifty-six years later, as I sat at Larry's feet with my head in his lap crying, "Lord, I want You to take me, too. I don't want to live without you, Larry," it was not hopeless despair I felt but a longing to go with Larry. I would not only be with Larry, but also the Lord. Larry's words of comfort and encouragement to me were in stark contrast to what happened when dad died.

The difference between the two responses was knowing and belonging to the risen Christ and the hope we have in Him. As Jesus told Martha in John 11:21–27,

> "Lord," Martha said to Jesus, "if You had been here, my brother would not have died. But I know that even now God will give you whatever You ask." Jesus said to her, "your brother will rise again." Martha answered, "I know he will

rise again in the resurrection at the last day." Jesus said to her, "I am the resurrection and the life. He who believes in Me will live, even though he dies; and whoever lives and believes in Me will never die. Do you believe this?" "Yes, Lord," she told Him, "I believe that you are the Christ, the Son of God who was to come into the world."

God alone made the difference, and I have the joy of knowing that my mother, before she died, knew and believed this truth.

I have sensed God's presence in a deeper way as He has showered and clothed me in His love and grace. He is always faithful. I may not understand His ways, and I don't need to, but I do know Him. I trust in who He is and know He never makes a mistake. He never takes us where His grace won't keep us. His ways are beyond finding out. His grace is truly sufficient. I also know that one day, I will be with the Lord and with Larry for all eternity.

I say "Amen" to Job's words in Job 19:25–27: "I know that my Redeemer lives and that in the end He will stand upon the earth. And after my skin has been destroyed, yet in my flesh I will see God. I myself will see Him—with my own eyes I, and not another. How my heart yearns within me!"

CHAPTER 8

Sustaining Grace

> Even to your old age and gray hairs I am He, I am
> He who will sustain you. I have made you and I will
> carry you; I will sustain you and I will rescue you.
> —Isaiah 46:4

> Tis grace that brought me safe thus far,
> And grace will lead me home.
> —John Newton

The Lord has not only saved me and is in the process of sanctifying me, but He is also sustaining me by His grace. I knew the Lord was preparing me for Larry's death. Several weeks before he died, I found myself drawn to John 11, the story of Mary, Martha, and Lazarus. It seemed as I read the story of Lazarus, words that I had read many times before jumped out to me—"Lord, the one you love is sick" and "Jesus loved Martha and her sister and Lazarus." I knew that was true for me, too—that Jesus loved Larry, our children, the grandchildren, and me.

Even when we knew Larry was sick and that the Lord would soon take him home to be with Him, we rested in the truths we knew about the Lord. Whether Larry was sick or well, we knew Jesus loved him and that He loved all of us, too. We also knew that God could make him well. But that was not God's plan for Larry's life. Acts 13:36 tells us, "For when David had served God's purpose in his own generation, he fell asleep." In God's plan, it was time for Larry to come home.

As I mentioned earlier, Larry died early Saturday morning. Saturday night, the children came to me and asked, "Mama, what do you want to do about church tomorrow?" I suggested since all the family was here (twenty-three total, except Bradley, who was back in Africa) that we have church here at the house. They all agreed, and the next morning, we all gathered in our den.

We had a sweet time together as Cooper (Brooke's husband), Joshua, and Nathan played their guitars and led the singing. Afterward, I shared with the children and grandchildren what the Lord had been teaching me in the story of Lazarus. I reminded them that even though we might not understand what God was doing, we should always trust Him because there is always a greater purpose for all that God does. Our finite minds cannot comprehend God's ways. He alone is God, and we are not.

Early in my walk with the Lord, I heard or read somewhere, "When you cannot see the hand of God in your circumstances, always trust His heart." I knew this was the time to trust the heart of God. Afterward, we just shared what was on our hearts, how much we were going to miss Larry (husband, father, and grandfather), what he meant to all of us, and the influence he had on our lives. I knew we would all miss his hugs, gentleness, wisdom, discernment, strength, and listening ear. He had always been a wonderful provider, and he loved his family. Reflecting on all of this, we prayed together and thanked the Lord for how He had blessed us with Larry's life and the time we had together. It was a sweet, precious time.

We all knew that our separation from Larry was just for a season. One day, we would be with Larry and the Lord for all eternity. In the meantime, I knew His love and grace would sustain me at all times.

Months after Larry's death, I woke up during the middle of the night and was talking with the Lord about the verse in Isaiah 54:5: "For your Maker is your husband, the Lord Almighty is His name." I said, "Lord, I don't know what that looks like. I know what it is like to have an earthly husband, but what does it look like having You as my husband? Will You teach me and show me?" I didn't hear any voice or anything and soon fell back asleep.

The next morning, I was sitting in my chair, reading a devotional book. The verse for that morning was Isaiah 30:21: "Whether you turn to the right or to the left, your ears will hear a voice behind you, saying, this is the way, walk in it." I knew in my heart the Lord was answering my question—showing me that if I was in tune with Him, I would hear Him speaking to me as my husband.

I said, "Lord show me what that looks like. If Larry was sitting here with me this morning, I would say to him, 'Honey, what are your plans today, and is there anything you want me to do?' He, in turn, would have asked me the same question."

I then said to the Lord, "What are Your plans today, Lord, and what would You like for me to do?" I didn't hear anything back, so I said, "Well, Lord, I'm going to go about what I would normally do today, and if You want to change my plans, that is fine with me."

It wasn't long before my phone rang. It was a young woman, Leah, whom I had been discipling for a number of years. She asked if we could get together because she needed to talk with me about something. I knew the Lord was in this and told her that would be good. I needed to go by my doctor's office downtown to pick something up and suggested we get together for lunch at one of my favorite restaurants in downtown Columbia, No Name Deli.

We parked the car on a side street, put money in the meter, and entered the restaurant. We had been sitting there, eating and talking for a long while, when I remembered the restaurant closed after lunch. When Larry and I ate there, I always got their raspberry or peach ice tea, and when we left, Larry would get me some to go. As Leah and I were sitting at our table talking, very clearly the thought came to me that if I wanted a cup to go, I needed to get it because they were soon closing.

As soon as I walked up front to the large urns where I got my own refills, it looked like the waitress was removing the tea, and I quickly said, "Oh, I wanted some raspberry tea." She had not removed the raspberry tea. I thanked the Lord for reminding me about the tea, since they seemed to be closing up, and went back to my table.

Within a minute or two, the thought clearly came to my mind, *If you don't leave, you are going to get a parking ticket.* I knew it was the Lord prompting me and thought, *I hate to interrupt her again.* Again, very clearly, the thought was, *If you don't leave right this second, you will get a ticket.*

I immediately jumped up out of my seat, grabbed my purse and cup of tea, and said, "Leah, we've got to go, and we've got to go this second. I'll explain later." It scared her, but she also jumped up, and the two of us hurried out of the restaurant. I turned to go down the street where my car was parked, and sure enough, there was a policeman standing at my car, getting ready to write me a ticket. I yelled, "Please don't—I'm coming!" Thankfully, he had not written my license plate down and did not give me a ticket. I said out loud, "Thank you, thank you, Lord! You are so wonderful!"

Leah was saying, "Grace, what is going on?" I then explained, starting with my asking the Lord to show me what it looked like with Him as my husband. As I was telling her, I realized that had Larry been there by my side, he would have thought about the tea and getting a parking ticket. The Lord was answering my prayer. Just as Larry had looked after me as my husband, the Lord would speak to me as well if I would just listen to Him. Larry cared about the little things that were important to me, like getting some tea to go and not getting a parking ticket, and the Lord cared, too.

Around this time, some dear friends of mine, Don and Loretta, invited me to the beach for a visit. One night during dinner, we were talking about Larry, and I commented how much I missed him. Don, who is a pastor, asked me, "How do you manage the loss of someone who has been a part of your life for so many years?" He hesitated asking me, not wanting to cause any more pain by talking about it, but I assured him it was okay.

I told them it was like my walk with the Lord. During the years since I came to know the Lord, as long as I stayed focused on Him and trusted Him to lead me, trusting in His promises, I was okay. But if I stopped trusting the Lord and keeping my eyes focused on Him, my walk with the Lord suffered. In the same way, if I focused on Larry and how much I longed for him and missed him, I started getting down. I understood the normal grieving process and allowed myself that, but I tried very hard to balance that and not to allow myself pity parties where I dwelled on how lonely I was and how much I missed him. When I kept looking to and trusting God, who loved me, died for me, and now lives in me, I did great!

Everyone grieves differently. I think it is very important to allow yourself time to grieve. Some days, I found myself crying at the most unusual times. I could be in the car, driving somewhere, and for no apparent reason, I just burst out crying. Sometimes I could talk about Larry and be fine, and at other times, just hearing his name would bring me to tears. That is how it is when you know a part of you is gone.

But the Lord knows my heartache and my pain, and He promises me His grace is sufficient—and it is. His sustaining love and grace keep me, uphold me, and give me the strength and peace to carry on until He calls me home. I rest in Him alone.

His Word calms and sustains me, especially when I go through difficult trials. Many times, I don't sense His presence at all. He seems very far away from me, and that is when I cling to Him and His promises the most. It seems like He hides from me; yet I know Him and His character. Even though this seems to be what is happening, I know He is there. He floods my mind with His Word, which reminds me that He is here. And "if God is for us who can be against us?" (Romans 8:31)

Often, we question what God allows in our lives or the lives of our loved ones or others. I know I have done that. He does not owe us any explanation. Often, people just get angry with God and won't have anything to do with Him. It is better to ask questions and dialogue with Him than to ignore Him. (He can handle it.) I know because I ignored Him for a long time. But that's not what He desires. God's invitation is to come to Him.

Before I came to know the Lord, I was one of those people who stayed angry with God for years. I felt like He didn't care anything about me and had allowed many unpleasant things to happen. I didn't understand why He didn't stop them. Why did these things happen to me, and why did I respond to them the way I did? If God didn't love me, then what hope was there? I left Him alone and wanted Him to leave me alone. I was very wrong.

It took me years to understand that He loves me more than I could ever imagine. "For I know the plans I have for you declares the Lord, plans to prosper you and not to harm you, plans to give you hope and a future" (Jeremiah 29:11). It took me a long time to understand that His ways were not my ways. When I try to figure things out, the Lord reminds me of Isaiah 55:8–9: "For My thoughts are not your thoughts, neither are your ways My ways, declares the Lord. For as the heavens are higher than the earth, so are My ways higher than your ways, and My thoughts than your thoughts."

That is where faith and trust enter. God wants us to trust Him, and we normally don't trust someone we don't know. That is why it is so important to know the God of the Bible. Knowing God and who He is is the most important thing—period! I know God's Word is true and trustworthy. It is like nothing else because it penetrates to the very core of our beings. It brings conviction, peace, joy, comfort, and hope like nothing else can. It brings healing to the soul. There is joy and peace that are hard to explain—they must be experienced. I am on a journey, and my faith is in the One who leads and goes with me.

In Mrs. Charles Cowman's book, *Streams in the Desert*, she says,

> In no way is it enough to set out cheerfully with God on any venture of faith. You must also be willing to take your ideas of what the journey will be like and tear them into

> tiny pieces, for nothing on the itinerary will happen as you expect. Your Guide will not keep to any beaten path. He will lead you through ways you would never have dreamed your eyes would see. He knows no fear, and He expects you to fear nothing while He is with you (158).

I am realizing more and more how true this is.

I've learned through the years that we cannot look at God through our circumstances, for if we do, we get a distorted view of Him. He seems very far away and small. But if by faith, we look at our circumstances through God, recognizing who He is and that He is the God of our circumstances, then we keep things in their proper perspective. I had to settle forever the truth that God loves me. That was demonstrated on the cross when He died for me.

I don't understand many things—but I don't need to. I know the God who holds me and says He will never leave me or forsake me. He is the great I Am. He owes me nothing but has given me everything. And what He has done for me, He will do for you.

John Newton, author of "Amazing Grace," said, "I am not what I ought to be, I am not what I want to be, I am not what I hope to be in another world; but still, I am not what I once used to be, and by the grace of God, I am what I am." I am very glad God has transformed my life and is still in the process. I am also not what I want to be. But I am not what I used to be, either. God does change lives.

CHAPTER 9

Strengthening Grace

> But those who hope in the Lord will renew their
> strength. They will soar on wings like eagles; they will
> run and not grow weary, they will walk and not be faint.
> —Isaiah 40:31

> When we've been there ten thousand years,
> bright shining as the sun, we've no less days to
> sing God's praise than when we first begun.
> —John Newton

> Life is a steep climb, and it is always encouraging to have those ahead of us 'call back' and cheerfully summon us to higher ground. We all climb together, so we should help one another. The mountain climbing of life is serious, but glorious business; it takes strength and steadiness to reach the summit. And as our view becomes better as we gain altitude, and as we discover things of importance, we should 'call back' our encouragement to others (page 470).

These words by Mrs. Charles Cowman in *Streams in the Desert* speak deeply to me and cause me to want to encourage others not to give up but to press on. Just as I was mentored in my walk with the Lord, I want to reach out and encourage others to seek that higher ground. This takes strength and courage, but God is faithful, and He will take us there if we will trust Him. My generation must be faithful to teach truth and not water down or compromise God's Word. Our children must be faithful in their generation, our grandchildren in theirs, and so forth until the Lord returns. "The One who calls you is faithful and He will do it" (1 Thessalonians 5:24).

Though I am now doing this without my life partner, for years God had been giving us the desire to faithfully teach the next generation through Bible teaching, mentoring, Sunday School, and informal counseling. Because this was what we believed, when we built our home, we etched in the concrete of our sidewalk the Bible reference Psalm 78:3–6. This verse reads:

> "What we have heard and known, what our fathers have told us, we will not hide them from their children; we will tell the next generation the praiseworthy deeds of the Lord, His power, and the wonders He has done. He decreed statutes for Jacob and established the law in Israel, which He commanded our forefathers to teach their children, so the next generation would know them, even the children yet to be born, and they in turn would tell their children."

When Larry retired, we took a few days and rented a house in the mountains to pray and ask the Lord to show us what He wanted us to do as we stepped into another phase of our lives. As we prayed separately and as a couple, the Lord just blended our hearts together with the same purpose. So we wrote out what we called our ministry statement.

Our *purpose* is to finish strong (2 Timothy 4:7–8, Philippians 3:12–14) by looking to God to give us strength and freshness to continue to bear fruit (Psalm 92:14–15), declaring Him to the next generation (Psalm 71:18) with love (Colossians 3:14) through teaching (Titus 2:1-8, Acts 20:20), training (2 Timothy 3:16–17), and testimony (Psalm 107:2, 1 Peter 3:15). Our *promise* is that our Lord Jesus Christ will empower and equip us for every good thing to which He called us for His purpose and glory (Hebrews 13:20–22, 2 Peter 1:3). Our *prayer* is that God will show favor on us and confirm the work of our hands (Psalm 90:17).

Little did we know then that within five years, the Lord would call Larry home, and I would be the one to continue on without him by my side. Since his death, I still look to these promises and trust the One who has been faithful to give me the strength and wisdom to see me through until He takes me home.

God has honored our prayers. It amazes me that at seventy-nine years old, I still get calls from women of all ages (but especially young women in their twenties and even some teenagers) who want to come stay with me or just come out for a few hours to talk.

I love it and know that this is in answer to my prayers. I want to tell the next generation and the next of God's faithfulness, love, grace, and mercy, and that He has no favorites. Knowing God is the greatest thing in life. There is no greater joy than belonging to the One who loves you and died for you in order to reconcile you to Himself. God's Word tells us in Romans 5:8 that when we were still sinners, He loved and died for us.

Even after we come to know Him, we continually need God's strengthening. Ever since that day in 1976 when I cried out to the Lord, I have constantly depended on God's grace to do in and through me what I could not possibly do in my own strength. He helped me love my mother and care for her when I did not want to have anything to do with her. He enabled me to speak publicly in spite of debilitating fear, to love others (even the unlovable), and to be the wife the Lord wanted me to be—even with my strong, rebellious personality.

Larry always told me what a testimony it was to him to see God's work in my heart as I yielded my strong will to God's will and how He changed me. He helped me learn to forgive myself—not only for the things I did, but also for the things I didn't do but believed I had. Through His strength and power, most of the time, I was able to be a loving mother and grandmother and good friend by speaking the truth in love. Only by His grace was I able to be humble as friends corrected me and spoke truth into my life. And most recently, only in His strength was I able to face life without my life-mate of almost fifty years. In all of this, I trusted God to do in me what I could not do.

I know there is a river of grace that flows from the throne of God, and as I drink freely from this river, God's grace abundantly meets my needs and satisfies like nothing else can. Even in times when I do not know what I want or need, the Lord knows, and He is always there, even when I am running the other way. God patiently waits, and at some point, I sense a still, small voice saying, "My grace is sufficient" (2 Corinthians 12:9). That is when I realize that this wonderful river of grace never runs dry; it is always waiting there for me to return and drink freely. It doesn't matter how long it has been or how far I have drifted away.

This truth is especially comforting when I'm hurt, lonely, disillusioned with someone, grieving over something or someone, or just need to be comforted. God tells the thirsty to come to the water and drink without any cost (Isaiah 55:1).

We may find ourselves in situations we never would have dreamed we would be in, or going in directions we never thought we would go. No matter what your situation, keep your eyes focused on the One who orders your steps and never forsakes you (Hebrews 13:5). Come back to the One who knows all about you, every thought you will ever have, and everything you will ever do (Psalm 139).

God is just waiting for you to turn from going your way to the One who loves you completely and unconditionally. You can just cry out to Him, for it will be His strength and grace that will bring you back. As you travel this journey of life, remember that God loves you more than you could ever imagine, and He has wonderful plans for your life. Your circumstances and people may seem to say differently, but He is the One in control. You must always trust Him, regardless of what is happening.

And now I am facing one of my biggest challenges—growing old gracefully. This will not be accomplished unless the Lord does it. Many times I heard Vivian say, "Grace, your walk with the Lord is a moment-by-moment walk." She was right. If I am going to finish well, which is my heart's desire, I must continue to look to Him constantly because I know (and God knows) I cannot do it. I must let Him lead. Exodus 15:18 says, "In your unfailing love you will lead the people You have redeemed. In Your strength You will guide them to Your holy dwelling."

There are a lot of wonderful things that happen in your golden years. The longer we walk with the Lord, as we listen and obey, He will grow us in wisdom and maturity. Age gives us a unique perspective on what's important in life and a reminder to invest in eternal things. The downside of getting old is that you cannot do what you used to be able to do and often find yourself having to ask for help. It is very humbling. It feels like I'm coming full circle—starting life helpless and dependent—and on occasion, I feel I'm headed back in that same direction!

Even in these past years through trials of health, I have seen the Lord bless me through family and dear friends: going with me for my monthly treatments, picking up prescriptions, and bringing meals as well as running many errands. My children and grandchildren really look after me in so many ways. One very special friend, Deb Brickle, has spent countless hours just listening; letting me "let it all out" like I would have with Larry. She and her husband, Artie, have wonderful servant hearts. Many times, she would sit with me during my five hours of monthly treatments and minister to me in many ways. She is a great gift from the Lord.

My dear friends, Frank and Sharon Kirksey, have spent much time making suggestions, giving advice for this book, and encouraging me to press on. I am especially thankful for my friend and oncologist, Dr. Joe Leland McElveen. He has seen me through some hard times and has taken very good care of me. It would be impossible to name everyone who has taken time to minister to me through these past years since Larry has been gone. The family of God is the most precious family you can have.

Recently, I have had some health issues that seemed to consume me. I was having one problem after another. Slowly, my focus shifted, and I realized I had lost my joy. Emotionally, I wasn't myself, and I knew something was wrong. I found myself complaining to the Lord. I struggled with this and asked my dear friends, Don and Loretta, to please pray for me.

The next morning, I was reading John 15:16: "You did not choose Me, but I chose you and appointed you to go and bear fruit, fruit that will last." As I began to ponder this truth, I thought back to when the Lord first opened doors for me to teach or speak to women, or when He showed me He wanted me to go take care of my mother and in faith, I went. I went wherever I felt He was leading me, no matter where He led.

I began to think about what Mrs. Cowman said that I quoted in the previous chapter concerning our ventures of faith. "You must be willing to take your ideas of what the journey will be like and tear them into tiny pieces, for nothing on the itinerary will happen as you expect." She reminds us that "He will lead you through ways you would never have dreamed your eyes would see." God wants us not to be fearful because He is with us and never forsakes us.

As I talked with the Lord about this, I began to sense Him comforting me and reminding me that even all these health problems were part of His plan for me. I was reminded again how much He loves me and that He is always with me. He showers me with His grace when I trust Him with everything He allows in my life. I needed to be willing to give up my plans and trust His plans for me. So I took a deep drink from God's river of grace. The journey is not always easy, but I've learned as I look to the Lord and trust Him that the blessings far exceed the troubles, and the strength to continue has always been there.

Why is it that we often don't cry out to God unless we find ourselves in a state of helplessness? Is it because we are always so confident we can manage by ourselves? I had someone tell me one day that he didn't want to bother God with things he considered to be insignificant. But he was very wrong—God cares about every aspect of our lives, and He tells us to cast our cares upon Him, for He cares for us (1 Peter 5:7). If He knows every hair on my head (Luke 12:7) and keeps His eyes on the sparrow (Matthew 10:29), then I know He cares and watches over me.

The Lord has been teaching me a lot lately about being thankful all the time. Yet that goes against human nature. How can you be thankful when you have lost the love of your life or when you've been told you have cancer? Yet God's Word says in 1 Thessalonians 5:18 to "give thanks in all circumstances, for this is God's will for you in Christ Jesus."

God does not take pleasure in our heartache and pain; yet He tells us to give thanks. The Lord is teaching me that He wants me to rest in His love and care for me and that I can truly be thankful in all things—not just the good things. I have come to realize that the more I understand God's deep love for me (and all His children) and trust His goodness and purpose for my life, and the more I rest in His sovereignty, love, and grace, the more I can truly—from the heart—give thanks to Him. It is not giving thanks for the hurt, heartache, and pain—but that I know, without question, that God is going to cause all of this to come together for something so incredible, that if I could see it through His all-seeing eyes, I would be in full agreement and say, "Yes, Lord, I agree." I believe it blesses the heart of God for His children to trust Him so completely. I have asked the Lord to strengthen me in my inner being so that I may always trust Him in all things.

The Lord would never call us to do things and not do works of grace in our lives to equip us to do them (Hebrews 13:21). I have heard people say that God never takes you where His grace will not keep you and be sufficient for you. I learned many years ago from Dr. Lawrence J. Crabb, author of *Basic Principles of Biblical Counseling*, that you need to set your mind on biblical truth, especially when going through difficult circumstances (72). The battle is in the mind, and God has said He works all things for our good and His glory. I may not feel like being thankful, but I have the truth of God's Word that is the basis for my giving thanks. My faith rests solely on God's truth. My actions stand on this truth, and in time, the feelings come. I don't focus on my feelings but on facts.

Staying true to what the Lord showed Larry and me about teaching the next generation, I have looked for ways through the years to spend one-on-one time with my grandchildren. Some of these ways include: driving them to practices, dance lessons, classes and ball games. I have also tried to incorporate fun times with them as opportunities to teach them God's truth. I don't force it; I just ask the Lord to give me those priceless moments when I can and wisdom to know how. As an example, when I would play hide-and-go-seek with my grandchildren (yes, we still played up until a few years ago with me in my seventies and them in their teens), we only had one rule. The rule was that you could not hide in anything (like a closet). You could hide behind a chair, under a table, or just stand in a corner of the room or middle of the floor.

Because I live out in the country, on a moonless night, it would be so dark in my house that you could not even see your hand in front of your face. We would use tape to cover the small lights on the computer and appliances because that tiny bit of light would light up that very dark room. I remember one time I decided to climb on top of my stove. The kids walked by me a dozen times. I was literally just inches away, but because it was so dark, they didn't see me. One other time, I stood on top of the bookcase, and they never found me. Both times, they didn't see me until they turned on the lights in the room. I know this may sound silly to some, but it was a special time for us. No parents were allowed to play. It was usually Benjamin, Sydney, Joseph and Rachel, and on occasion, we did let Aunt Deb play.

Whenever we taped over the small lights, I reminded them of the biblical truth that as believers, the Bible says we are "the light of the world" (Matthew 5:14) to those who still walk in darkness because of unbelief. When the room was completely dark, they could see that it took just a tiny bit of light to light up the darkness. So it is with us; we should never think we are so insignificant that our lives can't touch others for Christ.

In 1 John 1:5-7, we're told, "This is the message we have heard from Him and declare to you: God is light; in Him there is no darkness at all. If we claim to have fellowship with Him yet walk in the darkness, we lie and do not live by the truth. But if we walk in the light, as He is in the light, we have fellowship with one another, and the blood of Jesus, His Son, purifies us from all sin." As the day of Christ's return approaches, we need to walk in the light. As we do, we will help light the way for others in the days to come.

In the upper room, as Jesus approached His imminent death, He gave thanks and reminded His followers that He would soon be leaving them but that He would always be with them and would one day return. The Lord Jesus will come again. It will happen!

To my children, grandchildren, and the generations to come, my prayer for you is to be ready. Hide His Word in your hearts. Live by faith and not by sight. God is faithful. You can trust Him completely.

As I reflect back over the years, I can clearly see God's hand on my life. Would I want to change anything? Would I want to go through those difficult times again? I think something would be wrong with me if I said I enjoyed them. But being on this side of it, I can say I wouldn't take anything for being where I am with the Lord, and if it was the culmination of all those circumstances, heartache, and pain that brought me to where I am, and to know what I know about the Lord, then I say with all my being, "Thank you, Lord, for loving and caring for me so much. I love you, Lord." What amazing grace!

Until He comes or takes me home, I agree with Paul who said "Not that I have already obtained all this, or have already been made perfect, but I press on to take hold of that for which Christ Jesus took hold of me. Brothers, I do not consider myself yet to have taken hold of it. But one thing I do: Forgetting what is behind and straining toward what is ahead, I press on toward the goal to win the prize for which God has called me heavenward in Christ Jesus" (Philippians 3:12-14).